MY TESTIMONY:
The Battle Between
Faith and Fear

MY TESTIMONY:
The Battle Between
Faith and Fear

Joseph (T.J.) Smith

MY TESTIMONY: THE BATTLE BETWEEN FAITH AND FEAR

iUniverse books may be ordered through booksellers or by contacting:

iUniverse
1663 Liberty Drive
Bloomington, IN 47403
www.iuniverse.com
1-800-Authors (1-800-288-4677)

ISBN: 978-0-5954-5463-1 (sc)
ISBN: 978-1-5320-0885-6 (hc)
ISBN: 978-0-5958-9775-9 (e)

Print information available on the last page.

iUniverse rev. date: 09/29/2016

ACKNOWLEDGMENTS

This book is dedicated to my family, my biggest fan club. Throughout my life, my immediate, as well as my distant family, have always encouraged me to do great things. They've instilled a great deal of faith, hope, and prosperity into my life from day one. I love my family because the family is the strongest unit in the world. No matter what happens in life, let nothing come between you and your family. If you have animosity, strife, disagreement, or anything that is causing a broken relationship between you and your family, take heed from me and fix it fast. Life is far too short!

I dedicate this book to Sheila, my loving wife, who's been with me through the wind and the rain, through the storms as well as the sunshine. Although I've made a lot of mistakes in my life, my wife has always been there for me. When I think I am at my lowest point, she's always there to inspire and motivate me. She has never made me feel like I'm less than a man—even though there were times when I felt less than a man. I could never love another woman after loving her. Sheila is my heart, my companion, my lover, and my best friend. Had it not been for my beautiful and loving wife, this book would never have been written because it is a direct product of her years of encouraging me to write. I love you, Sheila, with all my heart, soul, and mind. You are, without a doubt, the greatest thing that has ever happened to me.

I also acknowledge my mother, Ruth Smith, who always told me that I was her heart. My mother felt my joy as well as my pain from the day I was born. When I started writing this book, my mother was alive. She has since entered into the Kingdom of Heaven. I know that she is looking down from heaven on this accomplishment and saying, "Well done, Son."

I dedicate this book to my son, Oronde, my firstborn, a miniature me. He's made me extremely proud because of his persistence and dedication to excel in life. My son is a strong man and a great leader. Oronde, I love you more than you will ever know. I give you my blessings!

The book is also dedicated to Christa Joy, my baby girl, who was spoken into existence. Christa is also my pride and joy. If someone told me he or she would design the perfect daughter for me in every way, I would say, "No, thanks. I have the perfect daughter in my baby girl." Christa, I love you more than you will ever know. I give you my blessings!

I want to acknowledge my grandchildren, Kayla, Devonte, Eden, Tristan, and Miss Zoey. In my mind, they are the world's busiest kids. They are a handful of joy and excitement. They call me Papa, which is music to my ears. They are the second generation of my immediate family, and I am so very proud of them. I love you more than you will ever know.

I acknowledge my mother-in-law, Mrs. Mattie L. Gill. She is a very proud woman with unlimited energy, and she has always been an inspiration to me. She is the most loving and wonderful mother-in-law in the world. She is full of wisdom and knowledge, and she dedicated her life to helping others.

I want to acknowledge the Ali family, the Gill family, the Joel family, Bishop Taylor, and family, Dr. and Mrs. Oggs, Dr. Jake and Lady Cheryl, The McClarys, The Prevo family, and the Underwood family. Thanks for all your love and support throughout the years.

I must not forget to include all of my cousins as well as my beautiful Aunt Retta and her family. I must also recognize Mr. Michael Lewis, a friend and brother from work who pushed me to complete this book for years. He was persistent in getting me to complete this book. Thanks, Mike (a.k.a. Master Chef)!

Finally, I dedicate this book to Steve in Tennessee. Steve was the best boss I ever had. He taught me so much in the business world as well as life in general. Thanks, Steve!

INTRODUCTION

I wrote this book because I was inspired by God and encouraged by my wife, over and over again. I was encouraged to write this book and many more. Had it not been for Sheila, I probably would have never thought of taking on such a task.

The purpose of this book is to give the reader hope, inspiration, motivation, and encouragement to pursue and win the battle between faith and fear. We are constantly fighting this battle. As human beings, we operate either in fear or in faith. I've learned that it's impossible to operate in both fear and faith at the same time. My purpose is to share a few chapters of personal testimonies about my own battles in this area. I hope someone will be able to relate to at least one of these testimonies and be encouraged. If you are going through some type of problem, you have adversity in your life or fear has taken over and faith seems to be taking a vacation, then you will want to see how I overcame fear and replaced it with faith.

My book is a firsthand authentication of fact with open acknowledgment. My entire life has been—and will continue to be—a testimony that will encourage you to reach out and grab the drive you need to get motivated to do the things you have always wanted to do. In addition, this book may help you to overcome a struggle that you may be faced with where fear has taken over and you don't see a clear path forward. This book is written from the heart with the mind to encourage and motivate readers to defeat and delete fear!

In the world we live in today, we seem to be faced with so much tragedy. Where there is tragedy, there is fear. In the past few years, we've encountered horrible events in the United States and around the world. We have to stop and ask, "What's going on?" From my perspective, fear is becoming the cornerstone of our society. People you would never suspect are carrying out acts of fear. Bullets don't have names—just missions. This book is not a recipe for putting an end to tragedies; it is a book to put an end to fear!

A person who leads in fear will capture an audience that lives in fear. A person who leads in faith will capture an audience that lives in faith. Fear is like a common cold; once you are properly exposed to it, you will catch it. Faith is like a woman giving birth; some can handle it, and some can't. Some women are in labor for twelve hours, and some are in labor for two hours. Is the process uncomfortable? Yes, but look at the outcome! I'm not saying operating in faith is always painful, but it could be. The key is to remain focused. When I was growing up, we had a saying: "The main thing is to always make the main thing the main thing."

I heard a minister say, "A herd of lions led by a sheep will always be defeated by a herd of sheep led by a lion." You see, a heard of lions led by a sheep will take on the leader's traits and characteristics of being humble and docile. Therefore, they will be defeated by a herd of sheep led by a lion that will also take on the leader's traits and characteristics of being strong, courageous, and fearless.

In the world we live in, it's imperative that we operate in faith. Otherwise, we will suffer the consequences of being defeated by operating in fear. People who operate in fear appear to give up all hope of ever being victorious. How can anyone live that way? People live that way because it's easy to cling to fear. By living in fear, you relinquish your powers to someone else. You forfeit control over your life, and by doing so, you give power to the enemy. The enemy likes it when you give him power. That puts the enemy in control. When you have the power, you're in control. He who controls the bottle controls the genie. Do you control the bottle—or should I call you genie?

I choose to live in faith. Faith is the winning formula because it's harder to live in faith. It is really easy to live in fear. When tragedy strikes, most people say, "I guess we will be next. It's just a matter of time." That is not a way to live.

Living and operating in faith is much harder because it is not as popular as being afraid all the time. People are anxious to share their fear with others who share the same beliefs. The formula for operating in fear is simple: you speak it! The formula for operating in faith is simple: you speak it! It's just that simple. The words you utter with your tongue gives life.

You can speak life or death to yourself with your tongue. You can speak prosperity or poverty with your tongue. You can speak residing in the White House or residing in a lighthouse with your tongue. You can speak working on a job with your name on your résumé with your tongue. You can speak working on a job with your name on your shirt with your tongue. You can speak working on a job with your name on your door with your tongue. You can speak working on a job with your name on your building with your tongue.

With your tongue, you can speak integration or segregation, education or procrastination, a prosperous nation or devastation. With your tongue, you can speak owning a piggy bank or owning a national bank. With your tongue, you can speak owning a hotel, a motel, or a Holiday Inn. With your tongue, you can live to eat or eat to live. With your tongue, you can speak owning a fish or owing the pond. With your tongue, you can climb the mountain, move the mountain, or own the mountain. With your tongue, you can speak words that will hopefully put it on someone's heart to give you rent money for the month. With your tongue, you can speak words that God will put on your heart to relieve someone of having to pay *you* rent money for the month.

Your tongue will give you the power to book a room at the Ritz-Carlton. Your tongue will give you the power to own all the rooms at a Ritz-Carlton, a Hilton, a Marriott, and the Waldorf Astoria!

Ladies and gentlemen, we are walking around with the most powerful weapon in the world. Your tongue is your life card, and f-a-i-t-h is the PIN number. How long will you carry the card around before activating it? If you want something to enter into existence, speak it into existence. Faith or fear—what's your preference?

CHAPTER

IT ALL STARTED IN SELMA

My name, Joseph, is a very common name and a powerful one. I was born in the small town of Selma, Alabama, and I am proud to call Selma my home. Some people remember my hometown because of the Civil Rights Movement of the sixties, and some because of other historical events. For me, Selma is merely where my life and journey began.

My mother, Ruth Smith, was a hard working woman. She was the foundation for shaping my character and Christian values. She was an exceptional mother, especially in light of the fact that she didn't make much money and never held a high position in a large company. She was a domestic worker who performed janitorial services in the same hospital, where I was born, Good Samaritan Hospital in Selma. When I was growing up, my mother did the best she could to make sure we always had plenty of food to eat and clean clothes to wear. She sometimes cleaned houses for some of the people with whom she worked to make ends meet in addition to her regular job. Can you imagine being at work with your peers and co-workers all day only to find that when you got off work, your part-time job was to clean their homes?

While growing up, we lived in the smallest house on Franklin Street in Selma. Our house was so tiny; I often thought it was a mistake made by the builders. It didn't bother me that it was a small three-room shotgun house because it was home, and moreover, it was the only home I had ever known with nothing else to compare it too. Our house was not very safe from a security standpoint, and that did bother me. Although, we didn't have any valuables worth stealing, most nights I was afraid when I went to bed that someone would break in on us. I felt safer when my older brother, George, was home because he was big and strong and nothing ever seemed to frighten him.

To this day, I still have dreams about the old house. Sadly, it was torn down a few years ago and only the vacant lot remains. The dreams I have about the old house aren't really bad dreams. They are actually dreams that seem to protect me from fear. Sometimes in my dreams, I experience an element of fear while I am trying to get to that old house. But I know that as soon as I get there, everything is going to be just fine, and I will be protected. In my dream I am no longer afraid when I get into the old house, and I experience confidence and the lack of fear. I had that same confidence in my big brother, George, when he was home. I knew I had no need to fear while he was around because he was my idol, my hero. We didn't have too much in common because he was 11 years older than me. Nevertheless, he spent as much quality time with me as he could in spite of the fact that he worked several jobs. He carried me around the city on his bike as if I was his little mascot sitting in the front carry basket of his bike. We went to the movies, to the park, and sometimes he would take me to visit his best friend, who called him "Big George" because he was so muscular. His best friend lived a few houses down, and his name was George also, but everyone called him "Little George", obviously because he was not as muscular as my big brother.

One endearing memory occurred when I was eight years old and my brother told me he was going to leave me for a while because he needed to get away from Selma. He said he didn't know how long he would be gone, but he would keep in touch with me. Soon after that, he left in the middle of the night, but he wrote a note prior to leaving. The next morning, my mother found the note. In it he stated that he was going to Birmingham, Alabama and he would go on to New York City from there. He also told my mother not to worry because he would write frequently and keep in touch. He never said in the note, or to me personally when he would return. I was in the 2nd grade when my brother decided to leave home, and we never knew why he left so suddenly. A few weeks later we receive a letter and a photo of him sitting in a room in Brooklyn, New York. He said he was fine and didn't want us to worry. Sometimes later, we received a second letter from him informing us that he was going to attend a major-league baseball game in New York. Maybe my mother just needed to feel that she was still connected to my brother George after he left us so suddenly. But regardless of the reason, my mother searched the television screen, looking for him among thousands of fans until I believe she convinced herself that she saw him. The truth is, we never saw my brother again. He was gone without a trace!

My mother worked in the housekeeping department of a local hospital known as Good Samaritan Hospital in Selma for many, many years. She didn't seem to mind because she was just happy to have a job. She never learned to drive a car or purchase a car. She walked to and from work, roughly three blocks, for over forty years. When I was seven years old, I had to get up at 6 o'clock every morning, get dressed and go with her to work because I couldn't stay at home alone. I remember she had to be at work at 7:30 a.m., Monday through Friday. While there, I volunteered to help her to empty trash cans, sweep floors, and sometimes dust before I was off to school. Since there was nothing dangerous in what I was doing, it was actually fun for me. This was something I wanted to do. I did more work each day before 8:00 am than any of my classmates did all day. The dedicated working habits of Ruth Smith were forever embedded in me, a principle I passed along to my children. To this day, our highly educated children have never been afraid of a hard day's work. After working with her for about an hour or so, I departed for school. The good thing for me is that as a result of getting up so early in the morning and taking on responsibilities, it shaped my work ethics forever. I can honestly say that not only do I know the importance of getting to work on time; I know the importance of just being able to work.

As I grew older, I worked small jobs in Selma for various people; jobs such as raking leaves, cleaning windows, painting rooms, and sweeping sidewalks. I was always on time for my jobs, and I worked as if I was working for my own company. My employers appreciated what I did, and as a result, I always had work. I had no problem sharing my earnings with my mother because we needed the money to make ends meet.

My grandmother, Pinkie Turner, lived in the house next door. She was a well-known woman in the community and very wise. She once told me that she received her wisdom from her mother because my grandmother was the 7th child of the 7th child, which was interpreted as a natural predisposition for wisdom. I know wisdom only comes from God, and He blessed my grandmother with abundant wisdom and knowledge. Truth be told, my grandmother and I celebrated our birthdays together every year because she and I were born on the same date in November.

My grandmother taught me many things, among them the importance of having a good education. She was so proud of my desire to learn and my enthusiasm about going to school. One reason was because no one in her immediate family had ever graduated from high school due to having to work the fields in order to survive. They were fortunate if any of them made it past the 3rd grade. So, her grandchildren and great grandchildren started a new phase in her life from an educational standpoint as high school and college graduates began to emerge. Although my grandmother wasn't a distinguished graduate from a high school or college, she had wonderful values, which she passed on to me. She had many grandchildren however; I personally spent the most time with her than all the others because of the luxury of living next door. She also modeled and taught me the value of respect. As a child, I was not allowed to speak when other adults were speaking. I was taught to keep quiet during storms while God was working, to treat others with dignity and respect, and I never gave my grandmother any back talk, as she called it. I received only one spanking from her, and that was for taking too long to respond when she called me from playing in the yard. Although it was only one spanking, it was enough to last a lifetime. It was not the pain from the spanking that I remember, but the fact that I had disappointed a woman for whom I had so much respect. The pain of disappointing one who loves you is not an easy pain to get over.

Like many other families, my family was spread out across the country, but we also had many relatives in Selma. I enjoyed the time I spent playing with my cousins as I was growing up. We played in the sand, in the fields, in the water, in yards and in the streets from sun up to sun down. To us, life was good. These early experiences influenced my thoughts about children. I believe children should be allowed to be children. They should be allowed to enjoy growing up and to enjoy learning the basic values of life. I also believe the family is the strongest unit, and families should always stay together as much as possible.

My first testimony lays the foundation for what God has ordained all of us to do, which I believe is to love. It all starts with finding the love of my life... It is the testimony about a young lady who eventually became flesh of my flesh, and bone of my bone. I refer to my beautiful wife, Sheila, whom I met as a Vacation Bible School friend when I was only 12 years old.

I can cause you to succeed, or I can cause you to fail. I can make you happy, or I can make you sad. I can work in your favor, or I can choose not to—for no reason at all. I can make you very successful, or I can cause you to fail because I am in control of your destiny. I can cause you to laugh one minute and cry the next minute and then laugh again.

I am always with you, and there is nothing you can do about it. I can make you excited, or I can make you feel low and depressed. I can make you feel dejected, rejected, and sick to your stomach. I can bring sunshine into your life, or I can make you feel dim, dull, dark, and hated. I can make you feel as though you have purpose in life, or I can make you feel as though you have no purpose at all. I can make you feel valued, or I can make you feel like you have no value at all. I am in charge, and you depend on me. I can be like a weight around your neck, or I can make you feel as light as a feather.

You don't know me as much as I know you—and, boy, do I know you very well. I can be cultivating, nurturing, and pampering, or I can be your worst nightmare. I can be kind and gentle, which works for me because I know you. What am I that you can't destroy, eliminate, reject, or cancel? What am I that you can't live without because I am there when you are awake and when you dream? I've been with you all your life, and I will be with you until the end. What am I? I am simply a thought.

Have you ever stopped to wonder how many thoughts enter into your head on a daily basis? I would venture to say thousands of thoughts pass through our minds each day. Our thoughts determine how we manage our days from a positive, negative, productive, and nonproductive perspective. We rely on our thought processes daily, and we take into consideration what others think of us. We are affected in one way or another by what someone else thinks. We think about our dreams and the effect our dreams have on us as we ponder how to interpret those dreams. We think about the decisions we've made, the decisions we need to make, or the decisions someone else has already made for us. A simple thought could change the way we live forever. It all starts in the mind. When you conceive of an idea, you must act by believing your idea in order to achieve success.

The thoughts that come into a person's mind can either make the person very successful or very unsuccessful. Once you get a thought in your head, you must make a decision. The decision will cause you to execute on the thought or not execute. Success is determined by a person's ability to make decisions. Some decisions are good, and others might not be so good. Either way, the decision has to be based on what started as a simple thought.

We often dismiss thoughts from our minds because we believe those thoughts are stupid or will never work. Stop to think of a few inventions that were successful. At some point during your period of reminiscence, you will probably say, "Why didn't I think of that?" Have you actually thought of some inventions and dismissed them? We've all been there at one time or another, but we came to a conclusion and dismissed the idea because of some form of fear saying, "It wouldn't work anyway. Why should I bother with the possibility of making a complete fool of myself?"

Fear prevents us from achieving some of the most desired things in life. I can recite instances of fear from now until the end of the year because I've had my share of operating in fear instead of faith or belief. A person cannot simultaneously operate in faith and fear. Just as two objects cannot occupy the same space at the same time, a person cannot operate in faith and fear at the same time. People often vacillate between faith and fear. The things we think about can cause us to miss out on blessings, promotions, money, jobs, friendships, and success. Fear can come into our lives at the most inappropriate times, but it is a decision we make and choose to live with.

I've experienced many things in my lifetime. Many of those things caused me to worry, be afraid, and even be concerned about my own safety as child. I grew up in the sixties during the civil rights movement, and I witnessed many things that didn't seem right to me. Why did people of color have to drink from different water fountains than people of noncolor? Why did people of color have to enter some public restaurants and doctor's offices from the rear entrance instead of the front entrance like people of noncolor?

As a nine-year-old kid, I traveled to various stores with my grandmother. Why did I have to get a diagram of my feet drawn on a piece of cardboard when I was being fitted for new shoes as opposed to being able to place my foot in the shoe-sizing tool that was created for that specific purpose? Children who were not the same color as me were able to do so, but I wasn't.

I witnessed segregation, intimidation, and humiliation while growing up in the sixties. I watched my mother being treated like an animal sometimes. I never recall her ever taking a sick day because she was required to be at work sick or not. She was not treated fairly, and as a child, I knew she was treated differently.

We had fear all around us, probably because of the culture of the era in the sixties. As a child, I think I worried more than my mother. I was worried about my mother having enough money for my brother and me. I was afraid we would not have food to eat some days, but we were never hungry. My mother always worked it out somehow. I worried about not having lunch money for school, but somehow my mother was able to provide me with twenty-five cents every day for school lunch because I didn't like carrying lunch bags to school.

In my later years, I came to the conclusion that fear is a state of mind. I don't care to have it in my life. How many times have people missed out on the loves of their lives because of a simple thing called fear? It almost happened to me at a very young age.

When I first met the love of my life, I did not approach her because we were just kids. She was nine years old, and I was twelve. However, when I first laid eyes on her, it was a crazy, young, weird kind of friendship at first sight. Her level of organization, attention to detail, and knowledge of the Bible was amazing. She had the respect of everyone in the church and she respected everyone else as well. At the age of nine, this very mature little girl was an assistant Bible School teacher at Ward Chapel AME Church in Selma. I immediately asked my friend to tell me all about her. I also discovered when I wasn't around, that this little angel asked my friend to tell her all about me.

When I first saw this little girl at vacation Bible school, I thought she was amazing. She was a teacher's assistant in the summer vacation Bible school. I was impressed by her level of maturity for her age, and although I never spoke to her when I first saw her, I made it my destiny to watch her grow for several more years—then I would make my move. Her name was Sheila, and we did not have any personal conversations because of our age difference. I made sure I joined her church, as well as every group; play, choir, and organization she was affiliated with so I could learn as much about the church as possible and one day become as knowledgeable as she was about teaching Bible classes.

From the day my best friend invited me to his church, I never went back to my home church. As time passed, we both started attending R. B. Hudson High School in Selma.

Fast forward several years in the future. To my surprise, I saw Sheila and her parents during a R.B. Hudson High School Homecoming football game. I tried to work out a strategy. I wondered how to make a move on a young lady at a football game with her parents sitting several rows above me? Fear took over, and my strategy blew away in the wind with my popcorn bag. I really wanted to sit with her—and not with her parents. I wanted us to sit together in another section because she was at the age where I could talk to her on a friendship level, away from her parents.

I saw us sitting together in my mind, and I could see our conversation being so intense that we would forget all about the football game. Her parents knew me because we went to the same church, and I was quite active in the church. However, her mom and dad were like a couple of hens hovering over their little chicks. There was absolutely no chance to fulfill my heart's desire of talking to her or sitting with her on homecoming night.

Fear got the best of me, and I just sat there with the agony of defeat. About twenty minutes into the game, the most beautiful young lady on the planet came and stood next to me. "Hello, Mr. Smith," she said. "May I sit with you?"

I looked up, and to my amazement, it was Sheila. I stood and said, "Of course, you may sit with me."

Although fear had gotten the best of me, Sheila did not operate in a fear mode. I looked back at her parents in the upper seating area and waved at them. They waved back to me. This was the beginning of a beautiful friendship. All my years of hoping, believing, and having faith finally paid off that night.

We continued to talk as friends, and a couple months later, she became my "secret girlfriend." We kept it low-key, only seeing and talking to each other at school or church. My friends teased me constantly, saying I was robbing the cradle because of our age differences, but I didn't care. I really loved her, and I knew she loved me. We wrote each other letters and exchanged them at lunch every day.

We didn't do anything to draw attention to ourselves, such as holding hands in public or making public displays of affection. After a couple of years, we went our separate ways. Sheila started dating other guys, and I started dating other girls. I tried to compare all the girls I dated to Sheila, and none measured up. Sheila moved to Detroit for her junior and senior years.

I graduated from R. B Hudson High School and went to junior college at Selma University. I took on a business major and a player's attitude—complete with briefcase and a pretty good line for the girls.

During my sophomore year at Selma University, my friend, and my brother told me Sheila had moved back to Selma. She was living with her mother, and she was "looking good." Although I was heavily involved with another girl (okay, a *couple* of other girls), I wanted to see Sheila.

Since my player's card had been activated, I said I would go see her out of common courtesy as a friend. The battle between faith and fear was raging within me. Uncertainty that we would ever get back together filled my mind, but my heart felt differently. My mouth told me I was not interested in seeing her, but my heart reminded me to believe what my mind had conceived. The principle here is this: regardless of what your mind tells you, if you want something badly enough, have faith and believe in your heart.

Finally, I got the courage to visit Sheila. I went to her mother's house and there she was. I thought she would be fat, out of shape, and undesirable from living the good life in Detroit, but I was so very wrong. My girl was fine! She was wearing a brown plaid suit in a very size small. Have mercy! When I finally picked up my jaw from the floor, I said hello. We talked for a while, and then I had to leave. I didn't leave the same way I arrived. When I left her home, I knew two things for sure. My player's card was about to be revoked, and I had to drop all the other girls I had been stringing along so I could work *hard* to get Sheila back into my life.

When Sheila returned to Selma, my whole life changed. She was my first real, true love, and we had so much in common. I hated that we had ended our relationship, but I was glad she was back. In my heart, I knew we were meant to be together. I really didn't have much of a plan for pursuing her.

Sheila was just so fine, and although I didn't want to think about it, I knew other guys would be all over her like salivating wolves the minute she walked out the door. She was *my* woman, and I intended to claim what was mine—what had been preserved for me for several years.

I knew how I felt about Sheila, but I decided to activate my player's card one more time to use up the remaining units on the card. In my quest to play the field, I contracted the flu. My doctor told me I would have to stay home in bed or in the hospital for a week. I made the decision to go home.

One sunny day, one of my girlfriends came to visit and see how I was doing. Anita and I talked while I lay in bed. A short time later, another girl came over to visit because she had not seen me in a long time. Kristy wondered why Anita was there. They had never met, and my intention was for them to never meet.

To make matters worse, a few minutes later, Sheila walked into my room. What a nightmare! I was in absolute agony. I was sick in bed with three women—who never knew about each other—sitting *together* in my room, steaming at me and at each other, and wondering what was going on. Sheila's prophecy was fulfilled that day, and my player's card self-destructed shortly after she arrived!

After a short period of time, Anita decided she had seen enough. She got up, threw her friendship ring at me, which I had given her, and stormed out of the house. About five minutes later, Kristy got up, threw her friendship ring at me, which I had given *her,* and stormed out of the house.

A few moments later, Sheila came over to my bed and decided to spoon-feed me some chicken noodle soup. Then she got up, *kept* her ring, and told me she had to leave because she had a date! You go, girl! First of all, she was the smart one to keep her ring. Secondly, she knew exactly how to get to me. Telling me she had a date was priceless, but it was devastating. When I got well, I crawled back to Sheila like the pitiful canine I was and pleaded with her to take me back. It worked, but she did *not* make it easy for me at all.

I was the big man on campus at Selma University. I was the president of the business club and president of the student government association. Sheila enrolled at Selma University as well, and since my player's card had self-destructed, Sheila was the only game in town for me. I couldn't afford any more girls—even if I wanted—because I didn't have the money.

During our lunch breaks, I often took Sheila to lunch within walking distance because I had no car. She would place her order, and I wouldn't order anything. She often asked me why I didn't order any food, and I told her I wasn't hungry. I knew all along that I could only afford *her* meal. I would have spent my very last dime on her because she was worth it.

When I graduated from Selma University, I accepted a job as an assistant manager at a fast-food restaurant. I also enlisted in the Air Force under the delayed enlistment program, which meant I had six months before I had to go on active duty.

At the most opportune time, I asked Sheila to marry me. The rest, as they say, is history because the woman I married is by far the greatest woman in the world. She is the mother of my children, the love of my life, and the air I breathe. I could never love another after loving her. She loves me regardless of my faults, pitfalls, downfalls, stubbornness, and shortcomings. We have grown together, laughed, and cried together, but she has never packed up and said she was leaving. I love my wife with all that is within me, and I want the world to know it. There is none better than my very own "Sheila B," my "Cute Girlie."

Actually, the first step to overcoming fear is having an abundance of faith or confidence. Light and darkness cannot occupy the same space at the same time. Good and evil cannot occupy the same space at the same time. Therefore, faith and fear cannot occupy the same space at the same time. A person must believe in one or the other.

Any challenges you are facing can be resolved by believing you have already overcome the challenges. If you are waiting for a promotion, a new job, debt freedom, or peace of mind, the formula for victory in every situation is to win the battle between faith and fear by claiming victory. Believe in victory— and you will achieve victory. Remove the word defeat from your vocabulary. Speak faith into existence in your life today!

Lessons Learned

1. When you live in fear, you relinquish your powers to someone else.
2. The formula for operating in faith is simple: you speak it!
3. Our tongues are our life cards, and f-a-i-t-h is the PIN number.
4. When you appear to have exhausted all efforts, trust your heart.
5. Life is not all about you. If you really love someone, prove it.
6. If you really want something in life, have faith and confidence in yourself.

7. The first step to overcoming fear is to have an abundance of faith.
8. Any challenges you are facing today can be resolved by believing you have already overcome the challenges.
9. Believe in victory—and you will achieve victory.
10. Speak faith into existence in your life today!

CHAPTER

2

A BLAST FROM THE PAST

We often find ourselves in positions where we have to exercise our negotiating skills in order to get the best return on an investment. When purchasing automobiles, we find ourselves negotiating with salespeople to try to get as much as we can for our trade-ins in order to get better deals on the vehicles we want to purchase. Some people really do their homework when they attempt to purchase new vehicles. They never give up on trying to get the bottom line down on the price they want to pay. When we really stop to think about the act of negotiation, we negotiate almost daily in one way or another without knowing it.

I took my car to the car wash, and two hours later, I returned to the car wash because the tire-shine solution splashed all over my car when I drove the car on the highway. I told the attendant I wanted my car cleaned and detailed again for free because the tire-shine solution did not meet my expectations. The unspoken negotiation factor was if the company had refused to clean and detail my car for free, they would lose my business. It was a win-win situation for the company and the customer.

I use examples of negotiations and win–win situations in this chapter to show how true negotiators never quit in the middle of what they intend to achieve whether they hold a winning hand or not.

Circumstances in life can cause a person to change his or her lifestyle and do desperate things for survival. People say, "Desperate people will do desperate things." Early in my military career, I had to get the meaning of being married, being in the military, and taking on additional responsibilities. I have faced situations that qualified as new and desperate.

During my first military assignment to Randolph Air Force Base in Texas, we lived in an apartment building the base built to hold four families. It wasn't Beverly Hills, but it was what we could afford. It was home, and it was available. The year was 1974, and disco dancing and disco DJs were very popular in nightclubs, bars, recreation centers, and house parties.

Disco music ruled between 1973 and 1980. I never really intended to get into the business of "spinning the platters" on the local level as a DJ. Since I love to talk, I always dreamed of being in radio broadcasting and becoming a popular announcer. I always pretended I was a famous radio personality. I recorded tapes as if I was talking on the air, introducing songs, and playing music for my vast audience. I played my own theme music at the beginning and end of my virtual radio shows.

I started spinning the platters in 1975. I visited the military Base Exchange (BX) store in San Antonio, and I fell in love with the most beautiful stereo sound system I'd ever seen. In the twenty-first century, we don't call them stereos anymore. Instead, we refer to our high–quality sound systems these days. I fell in love with a Sony sound system, and it was love at first sight. The stereo system was very expensive, especially for a person who didn't have very much money because of my pay grade.

I really wanted the unit, and I quickly put it on layaway. After several months, I was excited to make my final payment and claim total ownership. The stereo system was extremely powerful, and I could not wait to blast the speakers and see how loud the music would get. On the other hand, I really couldn't blast the speakers too loudly in the apartment out of respect for the other military tenants. I told my coworkers about my new stereo system, how powerful it was, and my desire to crank up the volume.

A coworker and very good friend told me to take my new stereo system and speakers to the base recreation center. Tom said I could set up everything on the stage in the main ballroom on Saturday afternoon when things were slow. By doing so, I could turn up the volume and not disturb anyone.

I told Tom it was a brilliant idea and took his advice. As soon as Saturday rolled around, I took my new stereo system, speakers, and accessories to the recreation center to see exactly what it was made of. To my disappointment, people were already practicing for a fashion show in the main ballroom. From what I could see, they required a lot of practice. I saw major problems with coordination while modeling the outfits, and they had no music to accompany them.

After watching their rehearsal for about an hour, I decided to ease my stereo system onto the stage. The group was only using the dance floor for their rehearsal—or what was supposed to be a rehearsal. I proceeded to do my thing and set up my equipment as carefully as possible. I finally had my system ready to test and waited for the rehearsal to end.

It seemed as if they were never going to finish. I decided to play some soft jazz, hoping it would run them away so I could have fun all by myself. Well, my plan worked—in reverse. Instead of leaving the floor, they started to get much better at modeling. I decided to change the tempo to a more upbeat style of music. I was sure upbeat music would get them running away, but it improved their performance even more.

I thought, *what have I gotten myself into?*

I talked to one of the coordinators, and we agreed that my music was the missing ingredient to the performance. I coordinated the perfect music to what they were modeling, including summer, spring, swim, and eveningwear. My music blended perfectly.

The next thing I knew, I was a part of a really coordinated and organized fashion show. The leaders of the show asked me to play for their upcoming fashion shows. I was excited about the opportunity to venture into uncharted fashion territory.

The fashion show group finally completed the rehearsal and decided to stick around to listen to my music. When the rehearsal was officially over, I blasted my music as loud as my new stereo would let me. It felt great. I played song after song, and I entertained myself by doing so. I was not really paying attention to the dance floor.

When I looked up ten minutes later, the dance floor was filled with people. It was four o'clock on a Saturday afternoon. I played for about an hour, and people came from everywhere to dance and have fun in the main ballroom.

The recreation center director came in and asked my name and how I managed to get all those people dancing and having fun with my music.

I said, "The people love my music as much as I love my music."

If I could repeat the same process the following Saturday at the same time, the director would offer me a contract to play every Saturday afternoon for two hours—and pay me fifty dollars.

I gladly accepted her offer, which pivoted me to the beginning of my new part-time DJ career, my claim to fame.

Fear and doubt suddenly came over me, telling me I didn't know what I was doing, I didn't have the right equipment, I would never be able to repeat my performance with the crowd, and I would be wasting my time. I thought about reversing the agreement, but who in their right mind would forfeit twenty-five dollars per hour for simply playing music?

I told my friend Tom about my potential part-time job, and he said I should go for it. He also told me I needed a "show name" for myself. He asked if I had nicknames when I was growing up, and I told him my best friend wanted me to have a nickname. He used the letter T in my name and called me "Joe T."

Tom changed it to "J. T.," but "J. T. the DJ" didn't sound right. So, he reversed the letters to make "T. J. the DJ." All of a sudden, a star was born—and there was nothing in my way except air and opportunity.

Tom told me to believe in myself and tell myself I could do it and be successful at the same time. I officially accepted the offer to become the recreation center's DJ every Saturday, and I took on the challenge of playing the background music for the fashion show.

When I took on the musical responsibilities for the fashion show, I really got involved with it. I eventually took control of the entire show. The fashion coordinators taught the girls how to properly wear the clothing, and we had a young lady who taught the girls how to model in a fashion show.

The combination of being "T. J. the DJ" and hosting fashion shows really took my part-time business to a new level. I called my fashion models "T. J.'s Angels." Our fashion shows drew packed houses, and we always had disco dancing right after our shows. I received free publicity from local newspapers advertising T. J. the DJ, and T. J.'s Angels would host fashion shows in various venues across San Antonio. When the word got out about my team, I negotiated contracts to play for most of the recreation centers on the military bases in San Antonio and the surrounding cities. I also negotiated contracts to play for civilian nightclubs and after-parties following major concerts.

The DJ business got overwhelming, and I expanded the business by hiring two more DJs to work for me. There were times when I had three shows going at the same time. Business was good, life was good, and the money was good. I overcame my fear of taking on responsibility and playing for crowds of people.

Although I made good money in my booming part-time business, I was starting to lose track of quality family time. If I could turn back the hands of time, I would have spent more time with my family. My son was born on Christmas Eve, and he was a blessing. However, I was so busy working my shows that I spent very little time with him initially. No matter how good the money is in your life, it is not worth sacrificing quality time with your family.

I performed Monday night blues Shows, Tuesday night jazz shows, Wednesday night "getting-over-the-hump" shows, Thursday night disco sessions, Friday night jam sessions, and Saturday night "anything-goes" performances. Sundays were supposed to be my off days, but I still worked some club or juke joint in the surrounding cities playing contemporary jazz music.

My work–life balance was out of balance most of the time. My wife and I would meet each other in the carport when she got off work and I was going to work my second job. I would make it home about one or two o'clock in the morning and start the routine all over again the next day.

T. J. the DJ was somewhat famous in the city. However, along with fame comes money, and along with money comes drinking, and along with drinking comes foolishness from being popular. People always like to hang around people who are popular on any level, and I was no exception. My friends were Jack Daniels and Johnny Walker Red. I never did drugs and never had the desire to experiment with drugs of any kind.

I don't blame Jack and Johnny because they didn't force me to associate with them. In my mind, I couldn't do a great show until I had consumed five or six drinks to get me started. The more alcohol I consumed, the more I would act the fool during my show. The more I acted the fool, the more other people acted the fool—and we all just had what we thought was a good time. Sometimes I would be so drunk at the end of the show that I would not have a clue about how I was getting home. Some mornings, I would wake up and look out my window to see where I parked because I didn't remember driving home. I fell asleep at a couple of traffic lights while driving home, and the cars behind me had to blow their horns to wake me up.

At that point in the game, my wife hated my lifestyle and all the drinking. The ironic thing about drinking so much alcohol was that I didn't really like to drink. I thought alcohol was disgusting. I believed my shows were more successful when I was practically drunk. I felt I had more control after consuming a few drinks. When I was home, all I could do was sleep because of my hangovers.

I am so glad I had divine protection during those crazy years when I saw myself as the star of the show. I had an agenda with the limelight, and there was no shame in my game. When I entered the room, I wanted people to know T. J. the DJ was in the house.

A few friends came to some of my shows. A couple of my homeboys were my neighbors, and they helped me to get home safely most of the time. Of course, there were times when we all got wasted and ended up in the doghouse with our wives. I'm thankful for my caring and understanding wife then and now.

I made a promise to God several times: if He would get me home safely when I was too drunk to drive, I would do better. I did better for a minute, but then I repeated my act over and over again. Sometimes I would show up for my military job with the worst hangover. Once, my commanding officer thanked me for showing up to work that day, but he told me to go home because I was in no shape to work. It was an embarrassing moment in my life and it opened my eyes. I never got into an accident, I was never pulled over by the police, and I never jeopardized my military career.

During my days of disco fun, I worked for a club about forty miles from the base. It was out in the country, and their specialty dish was barbequed pig's feet. On a Saturday night, it smelled very good. Sales were huge. This down-and-out juke joint was not one of my favorite places because of the distance. I accepted the offer to play when my entertainment schedule permitted.

I was driving home alone one night, and for no reason, my engine stopped running. It was two o'clock in the morning, and there were no other vehicles in sight. I was about twenty miles from home, and I could not see my hands because it was so dark. I tried to get my car started, but it wouldn't start. I decided to walk home to Randolph Air Force Base. I was wearing a suit and dress shoes, and the walk was quite unpleasant.

I was so afraid because I was in the middle of nowhere. Cell phones had not been invented for the average person, and my CB radio didn't work because the car battery was dead from trying to start it over and over again. I was reminded of all my broken promises. Fear dominated my life at that moment. I didn't know what to expect, I was afraid of the unknown, and I was desperate. I had no one else to turn to, and there were no cars on the highway.

I had a green station wagon, which I called the "Fish Mobile." It was filled with expensive DJ equipment and was on the side of the road next to a railroad track. I had no communication, visibility was very low, and I feared for my life. I ran for a while and walked for a while. It seemed like the faster I ran and walked, the farther the base moved away from me. I literally feared for my life from man and animal.

I've come to the conclusion that faith and fear are based on the unknown, but they yield the same expectations and results. Fear is terror and worry while hoping for the best. Faith is confidence and trust while believing in the best. Most human beings are subconsciously more content, to a certain extent, when operating in fear of the unknown. When you operate in fear of the unknown, you do your best to prepare for the unknown or let your mind drive you into greater fear. Words can drive people into a state of fear and panic. A person who is influenced by fear maintains very little control.

While I was stranded in Seguin, I had no way to communicate with my wife. I was sure she was wondering where I was and what was going on at two o'clock in the morning. I was not a Christian at the time, but I knew how to pray. All I could do was ask God to keep me safe. A person going into battle must maintain a high degree of confidence to have a chance of survival. In order to defeat the enemy, you must always be on guard. If you have faith, you will succeed and keep your mind focused on a positive outcome.

As I walked alone on an extremely dark road next to the railroad tracks, I had a chance to think about my life. I focused on the good, the bad, and the ugly. Suddenly, I made a decision. If I was going to survive my ordeal, I needed to take on a military mindset and start operating with extreme confidence. Once I made that decision, I was able to have a clear vision of faith. A wise man once said, "Where there is clarity of vision, there is acceleration toward the known goal." It's hard to move rapidly toward your known goal if your vision is cloudy, foggy, or not clear. Once faith kicks in, the fog lifts. The clouds move away and give you a much brighter outlook.

With my new clarity, I started to see one or two cars pass by. By the time they realized I was walking, they had already gone half a mile down the road. It was not the ideal thing to get into a car with a stranger either. However, I saw a dim light coming down the road from miles away, and it grew brighter and brighter. The vehicle seemed to have been moving slower than the posted speed limit. It was as if the person was looking for someone or something. I really didn't know what to do. I started to hide, but then I decided not to.

The slow-moving car pulled up to me, stopped, and a voice called out my name. It was my neighbor! My wife called Thomas and told him she thought something happened to me. She asked if he would look for me.

I was so glad to see Thomas. My car was about five miles away, and I needed to get my expensive equipment out. Thomas immediately took me to my car. He was pretty good at fixing cars. He took a look at my car, but he could not determine the problem. Instead of loading the equipment into his car, he told me to get into my car—and he would push me home. Tom was driving a new car and was going to push my old station wagon car back to the base.

I managed to get my car inside the gate and parked in a safe place on base. I will never forget when Thomas Matthews risked tearing up his own car to save my car and got me home safely. That is what true friends will do for you, and they do it from the bottom of their hearts. I made up my mind that Thomas would be my friend for life—no matter what happened or how far apart we lived. To this day, I still keep in touch with Thomas.

When that ordeal was over, I realized that fear consumed my body as long as I was afraid. I felt helpless, defeated, and afraid. It proved that fear and faith cannot occupy the same mind-set at the same time. When fear consumes you and you feel like you have no other way out—when the world seems to get darker and darker and you fear for your life—you need to find yourself in a quiet place and meditate. Fear is darkness, but faith is light. Light will always consume darkness. When you start to have faith in yourself and your situation, negative forces start to weaken. The positive forces take over, make your problems go away, and turn your bad situation into a good one.

The days of T. J. the DJ continued on a smaller scale when I was reassigned to Homestead Air Force Base in Florida from 1979 until 1981. In 1981, I was reassigned to England. My ambition was to turn the United Kingdom upside down with my fantastic DJ performances. The assignment in England changed my life forever!

Lessons Learned

1. Always have faith and believe in yourself.
2. Overcome the fear of taking on additional responsibilities.
3. Being a person who exercises patience is a good thing.
4. God will place people in your life, sometimes just for a season. Recognize those people and capitalize on the opportunities.
5. No matter how good the money is in your life, it is not worth sacrificing quality time with your family.
6. Remove the word defeat from your vocabulary. The only thing in your way is air and opportunity.
7. Don't ever let fear get the best of you.
8. People often vacillate between faith and fear.
9. When you follow your destiny, your dim light can become your daylight.
10. Whenever you encounter turbulence, sit down, properly secure your seatbelt, turn on the no joking sign, and then wait for God to move about the cabin.

CHAPTER

3

THE UNITED KINGDOM VERSUS THE KINGDOM UNITED

This chapter is all about grace, faith, and fear. Grace commonly means thanks. Grace is God's gift of love, forgiveness, strength, and mercy. There is no greater comparison in my mind than being covered in His grace and mercy. This testimony is a reminder that when we think we have all the answers, we are sometimes nowhere close to having all the answers. Situations that appear to be doom and gloom can quickly turn into pride and joy.

On January 20, 1982, my family and I lived in England. I was an active-duty member of the United States Air Force assigned to Royal Air Force (RAF) in Lakenheath, England. I really enjoyed my overseas tour of duty because I had never been out of the United States of America. England is a beautiful country with beautiful people—both inside and out. They really take good care of themselves. The stress level in parts of England is not as high as it is in the United States because the British people take teatime in the afternoons to forget about work and all the stress in the world.

When I arrived in England in 1981, my first day was memorable. I had to go to England without my family for a couple of months because of my rank. As soon as I found a house or a flat for us to live, I could request to have my family join me. When I arrived at the military airport terminal in RAF Mildenhall, England, after flying for more than nine hours, I didn't see anyone at the terminal to meet me. A feeling of uncertainty started to set in.

Fortunately, I had been corresponding with my sponsor, another military member assigned to assist me in getting settled in to my new military unit. I looked for my sponsor without knowing what he looked like. I hoped he would recognize me since I was the only person who looked lost. I examined myself and told myself I did not have the time to be fearful about what was to happen next. I had to come up with a game plan for finding my unit.

As soon as I put doubt and fear out of my mind and placed my thinking cap on my head, I saw a group of twelve or fifteen uniformed men heading toward me. As they came closer, I wondered what was going on. They stopped when they got to me.

One of the team members said, "Hello. My name is Captain William McClary, Commander of the RAF Lakenheath Field Training Detachment where you will be assigned to work. Welcome aboard." After he finished his introduction, the remainder of the group introduced themselves to me, really making me feel like a king. I was very impressed with my warm reception because I had never experienced anything like it before.

My sponsor introduced himself to me and helped me get settled in my temporary dormitory room. My first agenda was to find a home for my family, and they joined me two months later.

One of the military members was moving into a house on base and asked if I wanted to rent his off-base house. A policeman owned it, but he was on a tour of duty in Norwich, England. Although I was not a Christian at the time, God was opening doors for me.

My unit commander was a true and dedicated Christian and a very strong military and family man. He invited my family to his church for Sunday worship service, and we gladly went along. His church consisted of 100 percent military members who worshiped in a community hall every Friday night and on Sunday mornings. My family and I met so many great people. It would take an entire chapter to name all of them. My commander often took the time to witness to me because he knew I was not saved. He was quite patient with me. He never threw the Bible at me or tried to beat me over the head with it. His approach to Christianity was meek and gentle. He wrote the scriptures out for me to read. They talked of salvation and what I needed to do in order to receive salvation.

I listened to him attentively. I was still not sure if I knew what it meant to be saved or if I wanted salvation. I had a great deal of things to think about regarding the subject of salvation. Looking back, I wonder how I could not want salvation. Salvation should have been my top priority.

The Day My Life Changed Forever

On the night of January 20, 1982, we experienced one of the coldest nights I had encountered during my assignment to the country. The temperature was below freezing in most of the country, and we had snowdrifts almost as high as the door coupled with frozen snow from a few days prior. Icicles hung from the main entrance, and ice was on the ground all over our neighborhood in Bury St. Edmunds.

Our house was approximately eighteen miles from the military base, and it was fine because I had my 1981 AMC Concord DL. My new car had recently been shipped over to me from the United States. I routinely traveled on the British motorways to work, shop, and visit other military installations. We traveled to London quite often, so I was no stranger to the motorways, which are equivalent to freeways in the United States. When I traveled to work, a portion of my trip consisted of motorways, and the remainder of my trip consisted of beautiful country roads in the south. Some of the weeds on the back roads were just as beautiful as some of the flowers in the finest floral shops.

I thought about not going to work on January 21st because of the snow and ice, but I did not have the heart to call work and say I wanted to stay home. I also had a part-time job as a night manager for the officers' club at the adjacent military installation, RAF Mildenhall. I really needed to go to my part-time job after work. I followed my regular routine by kissing my wife good-bye and saying good-bye to my son. Little did I know how close I was to saying good-bye to my family for the last time.

After getting into my cold car, I got it started and drove very cautiously out of the driveway and onto the icy streets. I did something I can't ever recall doing when starting my car. I recited the Lord's Prayer while waiting for my car to warm up. I just felt the urge to pray before getting on the road, and since I really didn't know how to pray like the people at church with all the fancy words, the Lord's Prayer was all I knew.

While driving on the motorway, I decided not to drive the speed limit of 70–80 miles per hour, but I drove 40–45 miles per hour because of the weather and black ice. A British person told me the temperature could get so cold that the fog freezes, turns to ice, and settles into the motorways, causing black ice. I'm not sure if it's true or not, but I know there were patches of ice that could not be seen unless I was on top of them and felt my automobile starting to skid or slide.

After eight or ten miles, I came upon a slow commercial truck. I turned on my turn signal before going into the passing lane. However, as I eased my car out from behind the big truck, the person in the car behind me possibly didn't like me getting in front of him, especially at my speed. He accelerated to get ahead of me. As the car approached me from behind, I had no choice but to merge back into my original lane to avoid an accident.

As I got back into my lane, I was no more than thirty feet away from the truck. I immediately applied the brakes, not knowing that I was on a large patch of black ice. My car started to skid directly toward the truck, and I had no control. I could envision my car running directly under the truck, and I had no time to react. Just before making impact with the truck, my car turned to the side. It turned around several times, and in the blink of an eye, it started to roll over.

I never made contact with the back of the truck. As my car was rolling over for what felt like an eternity, I literally saw my life flash before my eyes—from childhood to manhood. I saw myself playing in the front yard of my childhood home. It was like watching a movie of myself being fast-forwarded, but there was clarity in each frame. I knew my life might be over, and I was afraid.

Fear was strong during the ordeal, but an inner peace came over me and would not let me die. The inner peace kept telling me to hang on and be calm. It would be over soon, and I would be fine. My will to live had never been so strong, probably because I had never been in a situation like that before.

The car was rolling, and items in the car were being tossed all over the place. I was afraid of dying, especially so tragically. I saw it coming in slow motion. I had to make a decision to cling to fear or grab the lifeline of faith. I chose faith because I had a lot to live for—and my job on this earth was not completed. Suddenly, calmness came over me. I said, "Oh God. Oh God. Oh God."

Something or someone took control of my car. It wasn't me because the only thing on my mind at the time was staying alive. I was able to release my fear while calling out God's name, which gave me hope. Hope gave me confidence, and confidence gave me the faith to believe I was not going to die that day.

I made up in my mind during the skidding, flipping, and turning: I was going to live. The car finally stopped rolling and ended upside down in the middle of the motorway. The car continued to skid upside down until it finally came to rest next to the curb. I unbuckled my seat belt, fell to the roof on the inside of the car, and was thankful the car had stopped rolling and skidding.

I was confused and tense. I thought the car was going to blow up because the engine was still running. I panicked and tried to open the door closest to the motorway, but it would not open no matter how hard I tried. I pushed and pushed on the door, but it would not open. I was trapped inside my own car, and that wasn't a good feeling. Fear began to take over my body again. All I could think of was being trapped inside my car. I did not know what was going to happen next.

I cried out again for God to get me out. There was no one around to help me on one of the busiest motorways in the country.

I had seconds to make my exit, but I was trapped. I saw no way out. I continued to push on the door that was not pinned against the curb, but it wouldn't open for me. A calm voice said, "Try the other door."

I kept going back to the same door, but it would not open for me at all. No matter how hard I tried, it would not open. The other door seemed to have been pinned against the curb because of how the car stopped. *Why would I try the other door? It's not going to open.*

The peaceful voice said, "Try the other door."

At that point, fear left my body—and faith came in. I knew I was going to get out of the car somehow. I took heed to the voice and tried the other door. Sometimes, we keep going back through the same old door that was once good to us, but there comes a time when what's behind the old door is not good for us anymore. When I touched the other door, it flew open for me. It was as if someone had blown it open. I crawled out of the car and up an embankment to get away from the car before it blew up. Fortunately, the car did not blow up.

A minute or so later, another car pulled up behind my car. A fellow military man jumped out of his car, ran up to my car, and yelled to see if I was still in it. From the embankment, I yelled, "I'm up here." He asked if I was all right, and I said yes. What an ordeal for someone to have gone through.

Within minutes, the British police and other first responders came to see if they could assist me. One of the policemen told me my car was a total loss just by looking at it. It appeared as if a very large giant had karate chopped the center of my car and crushed it.

I was shaken very much, and I was not sure if I was hurt. I looked like I was all right. The man who stopped to assist me took me to the hospital on the base to get checked out.

The doctor examined me and said, "You are fine. You have no broken bones or scratches." The doctor also told me that I should have been killed in the ordeal based on statistics. He turned on the news, and I saw that there had been several other accidents on the same stretch of highway. In all the other cars, there were multiple people. I was the only driver without any other passengers. All the people in the other accidents died that morning with the exception of me. I was the only survivor out of all the accidents on that particular stretch of motorway. It appeared that I died that day because it was the day I gave my life to the Lord. I was born again! On that day, I was reborn into the Kingdom of God. Fear took my life, but faith gave me a second chance.

What did I learn from the experience? Never take life for granted because your next breath is not promised. Live each day as if it were your last. Every day you wake up is a gift, and we should never take any new day for granted. Give thanks to God at the beginning and ending of each day. Just as people dream of what they would do if they won the lottery, we should dream of what we can do to help others.

Everyone needs to be prepared for the next journey. If you believe in the afterlife, where will you spend it? Are you prepared? As a result of my second chance—thanks to grace and mercy—I made sure I was prepared for the next life in the kingdom of God. I did the same for my family. Don't take chances with your life. Make sure you live life to the fullest. It doesn't matter if you are a billionaire or broke—life is a precious commodity. Determine what your purpose is on this earth. Once you are sure of your mission, seek to accomplish it.

You will be surprised by how things will align in your favor once you let the universe know you are on your mission and are determined to live life to the fullest in order to reach your goals.

Lessons Learned

1. Never take life or people for granted.
2. Sometimes, we keep going back through the same old door that was once good to us, but there comes a time when what's behind the old door is not good for us anymore.
3. Determine what your purpose is on this earth. Once you are sure of your mission, seek to accomplish it.
4. Don't take chances with your life—and make sure you live life to the fullest.
5. Everyone should be prepared for the next journey.
6. Ask God to allow you to be a blessing to someone each day and you will. It really works!
7. When in doubt, pray!
8. The only way to hear a calm and peaceful voice is to be calm and peaceful.
9. Sometimes life will flip us over and turn us around. We will prevail if we just stand our ground.
10. Always put yourself in a position to release your fear.

CHAPTER

ANGELS IN THE AIRPORT

This testimony tells the story of how an angel sent from God came down to save our son from getting killed in what would have been a terrible accident in an airport in Atlanta. We are extremely proud of our firstborn son. Oronde has survived all the ups and downs, roller-coaster rides, peaks, valleys, and stresses of life. He is not a quitter; he is a fighter. He always lands on his feet because he knows how to survive—and he knows where his help comes from.

After two years of my four-year tour in England, my family and I decided to visit the United States. It was the summer of 1983, and we were excited to take a vacation in the United States. Having never gone overseas before, we were anxious to share stories of our two years in England. We packed so many clothes that people thought we were not coming back to England. Our family has always packed too much for long trips because we sometimes didn't know what the weather was going to be like. We also didn't know how many functions we had to attend when we got to our destinations. We booked our flights on Delta Airlines since Delta was our favorite airline. We took along plenty of books, paperwork, and other things to keep us busy during the flight.

After nine hours, we touched down on American soil. I wanted to kiss the ground when I got off the plane. I was glad to be home in the United States, but England was not so bad. We had such a great time in the United Kingdom, and we looked forward to returning after our two-week vacation. We had no idea how much things had changed in two years. As we walked through the airport in Atlanta, we saw new styles of clothing, fast food restaurants we had never seen, and really cool advertisements for familiar and unfamiliar products.

An underground train took us to the baggage claim. It seemed like we had as much carry-on luggage as checked baggage, and the carry-on luggage was getting heavier as we walked down the terminal. As we approached the train, we breathed a sigh of relief because we could get a short break from carrying our bags.

The airport was extremely busy, but the trains did not have an overwhelming number of passengers. We were more excited than anyone else because we were getting ready to see family members we had not seen in two years. We had so many things planned, and we were wondering how we were going to fit all those things into our schedule.

My son was eight years old and didn't have much to carry. He was extremely excited, running free and having a ball. As we got closer to the train, my son got more excited, especially when the train stopped and the double doors opened. People started getting on and off the train, and my son stood by the entrance, anxiously waiting to get on. In his excitement, he ran ahead and got on the train.

He looked back to see if we would make it onto the train before the doors closed. The computerized announcement said the doors were closing. When my son heard the announcement, he looked at us rushing to get on the train. With all our bags, he determined that we were not going to get on that train. The train was going to leave without us, taking him to who knows where.

We started to panic because we were thinking the same thing. Without saying a word, he made the decision to get off the train to join us. That's when the real panic started! As the doors started closing, he tried to escape by running through a narrow opening in the double doors. The doors closed on him, and he was stuck in the middle of the double doors. He yelled and cried loudly as he tried to get on or off the train, but his little body was wedged tightly between the doors. The doors were crushing him.

He did everything he could to get free from those doors. To make matters worse, all the other people in the train just stood there and watched him. They did absolutely nothing to help.

When I saw what was going on, I dropped my bags, ran to the train, and placed my hands between the narrow openings in the doors. I tried to pry them open, but the train started to move. An alarm was blasting, and I was totally freaking out. I could imagine my son getting smashed into the wall.

I focused on trying to get him out. I was afraid. I was in fear for my son's life and could not understand why no one would come to our rescue. My wife was yelling for help and tried to assist me as much as possible.

My son cried out for both of us as he did all he could to get free. Have you ever been in a situation where you needed *now* faith? I didn't have time to wait for hours or days to cash in on my faith. I needed faith activation immediately. I yelled, screamed, and cried loudly for help in getting my son out of that horrible predicament.

As I continued to attempt to pry open the doors, I suddenly felt a sense of peace and quietness all around me. I could see my son screaming, but for a second or two, I couldn't hear him.

I felt someone hovering over my body, and I saw two long arms and a huge pair of hands come around my body to get in position to open the doors. There was a sudden calmness, and the arms, while leaning over me, placed both hands inside the double doors and pulled the doors apart like the doors were made of cardboard.

The doors opened immediately, and my son rushed off the train with tears of joy and pain in his eyes. We gave our son a big hug and turned around to thank the person for saving his life. But just as fast as the person came to assist us, he was gone.

My wife witnessed the entire ordeal, but she never saw the person's face. The tall, strong man disappeared into thin air. We never found him nor saw his face. We knew God sent an angel to save the life of our son that day. Our faith has always led us to believe we have angels working on our behalf consistently. Do you believe in angels?

Lessons Learned

1. Work–life balance is vitally important for your health and for your family.
2. Fear is darkness, but faith is light—and light will always consume darkness.
3. Never give up because giving up is not an option.
4. No matter what your situation looks like today, if you want it to change, you have to make it happen.

5. Great leaders don't panic under pressure. Great leaders prevail under pressure.
6. Never underestimate the power of NOW Faith!
7. Doors will open for you if you have faith.
8. People who live in fear will sometimes refuse to help others.
9. No matter how carefully we plan our future, we must always be prepared for the unknown.
10. Favor is not always fair.

CHAPTER

5

CONCEIVE IT, BELIEVE IT, AND ACHIEVE IT WITH FAITH

I relate trust to providing the correct information, doing the right thing, keeping a secret, not misusing information or resources, and being able to keep my word and my promises to others. A person of trust is a person who takes on a great deal of responsibility.

If you asked yourself if you could be trusted, what would your answer be? Are you a person who can be trusted? Can someone trust you with money, resources, or his or her life? When we look deep inside ourselves, these questions could be difficult to answer. I was always taught that trust has to be earned over time, and it is not something that happens overnight.

This personal testimony deals with a true test of faith and trust. Stepping out in faith requires courage. My wife and I had to really rely on faith in every respect of the word in order for this testimony to be written. When you receive a new credit or debit card in the mail, the card is just a piece of plastic with no value until you activate it. Once the card has been activated, the card carries significant value. We all have the ability to operate in faith, but if we choose not to activate our faith, it carries no value and causes us to automatically revert to operating in fear.

I worked for a wireless communications company for twenty-one years. One of the first things you learn about wireless devices is that if you never activate your device, it will be meaningless. The wireless device must be activated in order to fully utilize the unit.

This testimony applies to our knowledge of faith, and it shows how we trust God and activate our faith. You must have faith in something or someone to get the real benefits. Fear can surely become an enemy to your faith; are you filled with faith or fear?

The year was 1987; the place was George Air Force Base in California. The event was choir rehearsal, and my mind was far from singing in the choir on a beautiful Thursday evening in the base chapel. My wife was the director of the gospel choir, which consisted of members from the base and the local community. We had a great choir with very talented musicians, singers, and dedicated members.

On that particular day, we had a choir meeting for about ninety minutes to discuss upcoming events for the quarter, introduce new members, and discuss general choir business. Little did anyone know my mind was not going to be focused on a choir meeting. My mind was focused on planning for a new addition to our family. I wanted a baby girl in our lives because we only had my one son—and he was eleven. Originally, my wife and I decided we only wanted one child, but I changed my mind and wrote a daughter into the plan.

I pretended to take notes as my wife conducted the meeting. As the meeting progressed in an orderly manner, my first step was to think of a name for my little girl. Since my nickname was T. J., I wanted her initials to be C. J. I knew those initials would be perfect for her. The next step was to come up with a name that matched those initials.

I wanted to name her Crystal, but after doing some research, I preferred Christa. Christa means "the anointed." I had no doubt in my mind that her middle name was going to be Joy.

I had a two-week assignment at Nellis Air Force Base in Las Vegas. A beautiful young lady was assigned to help me get settled into my temporary job at the base. She helped me with office supplies, my rental car, my staff car, and my hotel accommodations. She answered all my questions about the assignment. Her name was Joy. I told Joy she had a beautiful name to match her personality, and if I ever had a girl, I would name her Joy. Joy means delight. Christa Joy was going to be our "anointed delight."

Christa Joy Smith was destined to be the newest joy in our lives. I had always wanted a son, and God blessed us with one. Now it was time for the daughter. I had a name, I had a visualization of what she was going to look like, and I knew she would run and grab my leg when I came home from work so I could pick her up and give her a big hug.

I had great plans for my daughter and could not wait for her to be born. There was only one missing ingredient, and that was informing my wife about my decision to have a daughter. My wife didn't have a clue that I wanted a girl or had planned the entire process. When I finally told her about my master plan, she said, "Who's going to have this baby for you?" I responded, "You are!"

Sheila reminded me of our decision to only have one child, but I told her about my change of heart. She also informed me that it might be another boy. In that moment, we both decided that if we were going to have another child, it was going to be a girl. We agreed to have faith and believe we were going to have a baby girl. Once we agreed to have this child, we had to activate our faith for what we wanted.

Later that year, we talked about the baby, told our friends of our plans, and kept the excitement going. We learned that it's sometimes best to keep some things to yourself. Your friends can sometimes put doubts in your mind and cause you to cast a shadow on the things you were excited about initially.

Fear started to set in. *What if we've waited too long to have another baby? What if my wife can't get pregnant at this time? What if it turns out be another boy? Will we be disappointed?*

When we were stationed in England, our good friend Herlena would always say, "You've got to trust God for *yourself*. You can't put your trust in man."

We quickly learned that faith and fear couldn't operate in a person at the same time. You either have fear—or you have faith. Fear causes doubt, and faith is the opposite of doubt.

Occasionally, we attended a community church with our longtime friends, Bishop Robert and Stella. The people were great, and the worship service was awesome. Traditionally, the community church held a "Holy Ghost Celebration," which started fifty days after Easter Sunday. The celebration was similar to a church revival and filled with church members, guest choirs, and guest speakers.

During the Holy Ghost Celebration, the senior pastor asked if anyone had a prayer request or needed prayer. At the request of Stella, my wife went to the altar and stood in front of the senior pastor. He asked my wife for her prayer request. She replied, "I want to get pregnant and have a baby." The pastor asked,

"How many?" Sheila replied, "Just one—a baby girl." The pastor immediately prayed for Sheila, and the stage was set in motion for this miracle birth.

A few months later, we went on vacation to Alabama. Sheila was feeling a little strange, and she eventually started to feel sick. We took her to the hospital at Maxwell Air Force Base in Montgomery. The doctor examined her and told her she was pregnant. We knew our prayers had been answered when we heard the good news. Our lives changed, and our faith grew stronger.

Sheila had a normal pregnancy routine and experienced morning sickness and all of the things associated with a woman's body being prepared for the miracle of birth. We purchased girl baby clothes and decorated the baby's room with colors, toys, and trinkets for a baby girl. We told our friends to purchase items for a girl if they were planning to purchase anything for the baby. Some of our friends laughed and tried to fill our heads with doubt, but we didn't let those negative thoughts enter our minds.

Sheila continued to work at an insurance agency in Barstow, California. She carpooled with some coworkers for a while, but she started to have complications with the pregnancy. After several visits to the doctor, Sheila was ordered to stop working and to go on bed rest to keep the baby from being born prematurely. She obeyed the doctor's orders and went on bed rest immediately.

With her not working, we no longer had a second source of income. Financially, things got a bit tough. I took a part-time job with a janitorial service to clean offices at night for a phone company. I should have known the magnitude of the job when the hiring manager told me I had the job before I completed my job application, which was printed on a note card.

Once the hiring manager discovered I was an active-duty military member, he asked me if I could start immediately. I said yes because I really needed the money. I reported to work thirty minutes ahead of schedule and received my cleaning responsibilities. My job consisted of cleaning floors and bathrooms, dusting, mopping, removing trash, and making the offices appealing for the workers when they came to work the next day. The only caveat was I had to do it all over again the next day at the same time.

I finished my first day of cleaning services around midnight. As I was clocking out, I saw two of my coworkers who were clocking out at the same time. I had not seen them the entire six hours of my grueling tasks. I was so tired, and I wondered if I would be able to drive the five miles back to my house on base. One of my coworkers said, "How was your first night on the job?" I replied, "Not well." She said, "Are you coming back tomorrow?" With a smile on my tired face, I replied, "I'm done with this job—and I am not planning on coming back."

That was the beginning and ending of my janitorial career. I take my hat off to janitorial service workers, including my mother. She worked in janitorial services for most of my childhood. It's hard work, and I am not the type of person who refuses to face hard work, but that was not my cup of tea.

I needed the money more than ever, and I didn't know what I was going to do. I was getting down to nothing financially. My military pay was good, but I couldn't make ends meet with just one income. I started praying for a part-time job where I could work, make decent money, and have the flexibility to get to my wife in a short period of time if needed.

A few days later, I received a call from a sergeant I didn't really know. He said someone told him I was looking for a great part-time job, and he believed he had just the job I was looking for. He had seen me on the base, and he knew my supervisor. He saw me as a man of integrity and a man who needed a part-time job. He was head of security at a department store, and he needed another part-time loss-prevention security officer.

I really had no experience as a security officer, but I was willing to give it a shot. The gentleman told me he would teach me all I needed to know. I went to see him at the department store, completed the application, and waited for my background check to return.

A few days later, he asked if I was ready to go to work as a part-time security officer. I accepted the job with joy in my heart and a sense of uncertainty.

My new supervisor taught me the ropes of undercover security in a department store. I had no idea there were so many dishonest people who went into stores to steal. The reality was that we would never catch all of them. The pay was great, the hours were fantastic, and the employees were the best. This company believed in providing outstanding customer service to internal and external customers, and they did it very well.

Once I had a great part-time job, we could once again make ends meet financially. Now, it was all about my baby girl. My wife still had complications, and on April 19, 1988, Sheila went into labor. I had been in the delivery room for the birth of my son, and I surely didn't want to miss out on the miracle birth of my daughter.

After a few hours of labor at George Air Force Base Hospital in Victorville, California, my wife gave birth to a screaming and beautiful baby girl. The doctor gave me the honor of cutting the umbilical cord. Christa Joy was immediately cleaned by a nurse and given to me to hold for the first time. I took my daughter over to the area for feeding and had the honor of giving my daughter her first bottle. I couldn't take my eyes off this little angel and thanked God for her birth.

Christa and I spent about an hour together before I remembered that her mother hadn't seen her at all. I was so excited about our little baby that I'd completely forgotten about the person who'd done all the hard work to get her here. When Sheila finally got a chance to see our daughter, she did what all mothers do. She counted her fingers and toes, checked her out from head to toe, and smiled at me as if to say, "The pain was worth it."

When I got home from the hospital, I called everyone I knew to tell them the good news.

My friends started to say, "Well, T. J., you said it was going to be a girl, and I guess you were right."

When you activate your faith for something and really believe it's going to take place, all you need to do from the activation point is to expect it to happen. My wife and I called her the faith baby because she is a living witness of what you can achieve if you activate your faith.

Lessons Learned

1. Don't let people talk you out of your blessing.
2. If you are a person of integrity, people will know it by your actions.
3. Sometimes life will deal you a hand you don't like. Remember that you are not in control of your life. Against all odds, make that hand a winning hand.

4. Fear causes doubt, and faith is the opposite of doubt.
5. If you want it, speak it into existence.
6. Conceive it, believe it, and achieve it!
7. Never underestimate the power of prayer.
8. Stop existing in doubt…start living in confidence.
9. Make a decision and stick to it.
10. Don't let others cause you to get in your own way.

CHAPTER
6
BROKEN—BUT NOT DESTROYED

If I am dealing with a multitude of problems, how can I possibly find encouragement? The Lord might allow you to gain strength through meeting an unexpected person. One of my best friends, Bishop Robert Taylor, is the pastor of a very large church in Oklahoma. He once preached a sermon about how someone can be encouraged. The title of the sermon was "I Am Somebody." I heard his sermon more than twenty years ago, but I still remember the Sunday he preached it. I consistently refer back to that message when I need encouragement today. I don't believe anyone is free from problems.

When I think of a man of integrity, I can't help but think of Job in the Bible. I refer to Job in this book because of his great love and respect for God. I am truly encouraged by Job and his ability to withstand the trials and tribulations he endured in his lifetime.

We have gone—and we will continue to go—through life's daily challenges in our homes and at our jobs. However, we must be encouraged to continue the fight to overcome challenges and forces that try to cause us harm or set us back. When we don't have anyone to encourage us, we must encourage ourselves.

I speak about integrity in this testimony because it took a great deal of submission, humility, dedication, and integrity to get through this encounter. I had to go through a storm, and I wanted to give up many times. I wanted to pull to the side of the road or turn around. I've learned how we must encounter three types of storms. There is the storm we are currently facing, the storm we just encountered, and the storm that's currently brewing in a faraway ocean.

The storm we are currently facing can be unpredictable. If you know it's going to storm, you carry an umbrella and dress for the rain, sleet, snow, wind, water, hail, or ice. The fallout from the storm can be devastating if we fail to properly prepare for it. An umbrella may work on a windy day in Selma, but the same umbrella may not hold up in windy conditions in Chicago, New York, or London because atmospheric conditions can differ significantly.

I've been faced with all those storms numerous times, especially in this next testimony. Problems can be solved and encouragement can be yours if you have faith. Faith requires patience and holding on even when times seem impossible. I've been there, and I know faith, when activated, works. If you know your faith is dormant, I encourage you to quickly jump-start your faith into activation.

Once upon a time, not so long ago, in a land not so far away, I worked for a very prestigious and upscale department store in Montgomery, Alabama. I sold ladies' shoes ... yes, ladies' shoes. The year was 1994, and the month was January. I had just transitioned from the United States Air Force, and I was looking for work in the civilian world.

Just before I retired from the air force, I sent a prayer request to God containing the things I wanted Him to do for me upon my arrival in Selma. I wanted to have a good job, making good money, and I wanted to travel a little. I also wanted to take thirty days off because I had been working for twenty years, four months, and twenty-one days in the United States Air Force. I never had thirty days off consecutively during my air force career. I never mentioned where I wanted to live or what type automobile I wanted to drive. I specifically said I wanted to make good money and not great money. When you ask God for something, you had better be more specific than I was because you just might get what you ask for.

My family and I arrived in Selma in November 1993, and we went directly to my mother-in-law's home to stay with her for a short time. I am thankful for my mother-in-law, Mrs. Mattie L. Gill, because she is a woman of God. Had it not been for her, I would not have the wonderful wife I have today.

Prior to arriving in Selma, we spent Thanksgiving in Oklahoma with some of our best friends. We enjoyed a feast fit for kings and queens at the home of Bishop Robert and Stella Taylor. I believe the Taylors wrote the book on hospitality because we were totally comfortable and relaxed in their home. We arrived in Selma during a very cold winter. After we got our luggage unpacked and settled into our room at my mother-in-law's home, I sat on the bed with my wife. I felt helpless. I shed a few tears because, for the first time in twenty years, I was without a job. I had saved up about eighty vacation days—the military calls it terminal leave—which allowed me to process out and depart from the base early. I received full active-duty pay until my official retirement date of January 31, 1994.

One of the best things I did when traveling to Alabama was to take my computer and laser printer with me. Our major household goods had been shipped to a designated location and placed in a holding area until we found a home. Once the mission was accomplished, we could have our household goods shipped to our new address. I stayed up night after night, working on my résumé and sending it to as many companies as I could think of between Montgomery and Atlanta. My wife and I talked about living in Atlanta during my twenty-year air force career and hoped one day to make Atlanta our home. I had issues because I had no job, and I had not done a good job of saving any money to accommodate the transition. Although I had some money, I could see it wasn't going to last very long.

For the entire month of December, I sent out résumés. I did not get any responses—not even an offer to wash dishes. I was getting frustrated and afraid of the unknown. Fear was dominant in my life at the time because I had been faced with a situation I had not been faced with in a long time. I had more to think about than myself. I had a family to support. My wife and I departed from the house every day as if we were going to work, but we were just looking for work, hoping at least one of us would land a job.

I grew more frustrated because I was not getting any responses from my résumés. When I was just about at the point of wanting to explode with fear and frustration, I went back to God with a desperate plea to explain why I was not getting any job offers. I was desperate for an answer, and I needed answers for my sanity's sake.

As I was praying, I was reminded of how I had asked for thirty days off. For thirty days in December, I got no responses because

I was supposed to be resting until the New Year. This response blew my mind; I didn't know what to do for a moment. With that revelation, I felt peace in my life. My faith started to kick in again. I tried to balance my fear and faith so my fear would gradually leave and my faith would rapidly increase. Fear had to leave before faith could take control. Trying to live with fear and faith at the same time is like trying to make two objects occupy the same space at the same time; the concept doesn't work.

As a result of this good news from above, faith took control of my life. I decided to enjoy Christmas with my family. We had a good holiday season, and we were so thankful. We traveled safely across the Mohave Desert to get to Alabama without incident or accident. We had good transportation, life, health, and strength. Most of all, we had each other as a family.

As soon as 1994 arrived (the thirty-first day), I started to receive all types of responses to my résumés. Most of the responses were canned letters thanking me for applying and stating my résumé would remain on file to be matched against future openings. I was a bit disappointed that I didn't get any positive responses from any of the major companies, but my faith was still intact and activated. My wife and I continued to pursue our daily routine of looking for work from early in the mornings to late in the evenings. My wife had two good dresses, and she alternated them for job interviews. I had three good suits: black, gray, and a black-and-gray combination of the two suits I owned. Having worn a military uniform for twenty years, I didn't purchase many civilian suits. My civilian wardrobe was slim to none with the exception of casual clothing. As time moved on, we found an apartment to rent in Montgomery, and we were excited to get our own space.

When we got approval to move into the Carriage Hills Apartments in Montgomery, my wife and I continued our job searches. I finally landed a part-time job at the Base Exchange on one of the military bases in Montgomery. The job was great, and the people were wonderful, but I didn't get too many hours since it was just after the holiday season.

I continued to pursue my career, and I applied for a supervisor or manager's job at one of the major anchor stores in the mall. I finally received a positive response and an interview, which was the break I was looking for. People say you can't find a job until you get a job, and the theory seemed to have proven true in my case particularly. When I went in for the interview, the human resources manager told me they had an opening in the ladies' shoe department, but it was strictly commission. I could work forty hours per week and make as much money as I could make, based on retail sales of shoes and accessories. Disappointed that I didn't get a manager or supervisor's job right away, I accepted the offer.

Some people say, "If a man doesn't work, he shouldn't eat." I wondered about my prayer request to land a good job. I was reminded that I wasn't specific in what type of job I wanted or the amount of money I wanted to make. I wanted to think I was being tested, but I realized I was getting exactly what I asked for. I humbled myself and decided to do the best job I could, selling ladies' shoes for the first time in my life.

The store wanted to know if I was willing to sell shoes, and they apparently realized my drive and ambition when they hired me. For an entire week, I received training on how to provide exceptional customer service and sell shoes and accessories. I learned how shoes were made and received training on the point-of-sale system and inventory control.

I knew God was probably testing me because I started at the feet. He wanted to see if I was worthy enough to move up from the feet to the head. I interpreted it as moving from the bottom to the top in my career.

I had some embarrassing moments when my friends and high school classmates came into the store and saw me selling shoes. Some of my friends had moved from Selma to Montgomery, and some of them were working at very prestigious jobs based on their dress and appearance. To make matters worse, at lunchtime, many air force members in uniform came through the shopping mall doors. I felt deeply hurt inside because I was no longer on active military duty.

The first 120 days of being out of the air force and transitioning into civilian life was one of the toughest challenges I'd ever faced. Nevertheless, I pressed on. I knew there was a higher calling for me down the road if I could stick it out for a while with my current job of selling ladies shoes. My commission was approximately 10 percent on the retail price of each pair of shoes I sold, which was great. However, if the customer returned the shoes, I would lose my commission.

I never knew what amount I would be paid from week to week, but I was so thankful to have a job with a company where I saw promotion opportunities all around me. I needed to stop living in the past and thinking of my military life when I was the boss and had people working for me. I called the shots, made decent money, and never had to worry about not having enough to feed my family.

Living in the past was hindering my progression for the future. I started to complain. I came to the conclusion that I needed to take inventory of my life and determine what was working for me and discard what was not working in my favor. If you want to maximize your life, learn to let the good days outweigh the bad days—and be thankful that you are still above ground. Things could always be worse. I wanted things to happen quickly. I needed to learn and master my job in order to position myself for career progression.

When I complained about my humiliation in the shoe department, God told me he would promote me when I started to enjoy my job. I took that response and ran with it. I *pretended* with all my heart to love my job, but God saw right through my plan.

I was responsible for dusting and displaying all the name-brand shoes in an appealing fashion. Selling shoes, especially ladies' shoes, was like cooking macaroni and cheese. To my knowledge, no one I know has ever tasted macaroni and cheese to see how good it was and overlooked the appearance. The first thing people do when they see macaroni and cheese is look at its appearance, texture, and color. If it's runny, soggy, and floating around the dish, most people will simply walk past the unappealing dish. However, when a macaroni and cheese dish looks like Sheila B.'s macaroni and cheese, which is infused with a deep yellow color from using the finest cheese, nice texture, and a tiny bit dark around the edges—just enough to say eat me now—that's appealing and darn good for the mind, body, and soul. My shoe islands always looked great and appealed to women and men.

One of my customers would come to the store approximately every six weeks and purchase two pairs of the same shoes—one pair for his wife and one pair for his "sidepiece." I appreciated the sale and stayed out of his personal business. I started to make pretty good money once I learned the ropes and watched the other professionals in the department. I loved when the ladies purchased shoes and matching handbags because it was a great commission for me. Since I was required to wear a suit on the job, I was able to take advantage of some really great suit sales with my 40 percent employee discount.

As time moved on, I really started to settle in and enjoy my job. My supervisor started talking to me about being in charge of a very expensive shoe line we were starting to carry, and she enrolled me in training classes to learn more about the brand so I could teach the others in my department. We had company-sponsored fashion shows several times per year, which kept our employees abreast of the latest trends in the fashion world. We wore seasonal clothing at various intervals, and our customers really enjoyed seeing us dress so well. One of my customers wanted to purchase the clothes off my back because he liked the coordination. On the other hand, I had nothing in the way of fine suits compared to others in my department, especially my friend who was in the United States Air Force Reserves. He could wear coordinated clothing combinations that would make you cry in excitement.

One day, a coworker asked if I would watch his section in the men's shoe department for an hour while he went to lunch. He had asked numerous coworkers in other departments, but he got no takers. I told him I would gladly watch his department while he enjoyed his lunch. During the hour I worked in men's shoes, a distinguished gentleman came to the shoe department. He was talking on a cellular phone and looking as if he had just stepped out of GQ.

I decided I wanted a cell phone as well, but I could not afford one at the time. The gentleman asked if I would show him some of our top-of-the-line shoes so he could compare them before making his decision. I assisted him with care, using my exceptional customer service skills—just as I did with all my customers.

A simple touch of professionalism left a lasting impression on my customer. He purchased two pairs of very expensive shoes. He also said he had two boys and wanted to purchase basketball shoes for them. I told him that the shoes would be on sale in a couple of days, and he could get a 40 percent discount if he waited. I told him I would make sure he got his shoes with the sale price if he came back when the sale started.

The customer thanked me and said he would come back during the sale. I gave him his dress shoes, and he departed as a satisfied customer. A few days later, he returned and bought the basketball shoes I was holding for him. He was so grateful for my act of kindness and promised to give us repeat business.

I continued to pursue my career advancement by responding to tempting ads in the classified section of the local newspaper. I wanted a career instead of a job. Finally, I saw an ad in for an administrative assistant at the Cellular One retail store in Montgomery. I had four degrees at the time and was seeking my fifth degree. I knew I had the credentials to be an administrative assistant for this fast-growing company. My goal was to get my foot in the door. If I could get on board in the wireless industry, I would eventually work my way up the corporate ladder.

I applied for the job, and to my surprise, I was offered an interview. I prepared for the interview by studying potential questions, picking out the right suit, and covering all my bases. When I arrived for the interview, the receptionist introduced me to the executive vice president of the parent company that owned Cellular One in the Southeast. Steve wanted to hire an administrative assistant for his office. We talked for a few minutes, and he told me I was extremely overqualified for the job, but he liked my résumé and drive. He decided to send my résumé to the manager of the Cellular One retail store, which happened to be in the same building. He wanted me to interview with the store manager because he was impressed with my military, management, and educational background. He knew the manager was looking for a service manager for the technical services department, and he wanted to get my name in the pot.

I had no cellular experience, but I did have management and communication experience. The vice president was not the hiring manager, but he would see to it that I was given an interview. He escorted me to the hiring manager's administrative assistant's desk and formally introduced me. He asked her to get me on the list to be interviewed for the service manager's position. The administrative assistant said she would honor his request, but there were thirteen applicants ahead of me.

As we were about to leave, the hiring manager's door opened and one of the applicants exited the office. Steve said he would introduce me to the hiring manager since he was available at moment. Needless to say, that moment was the pivotal point in my life and my career. That was the moment when faith and promise were in the same place at the same time. Faith and promise—not faith and fear.

When we opened the door to the office, it was the distinguished gentleman from the department store. Mr. Smith said, "I know this guy. He works at the department store in the mall, and he provides exceptional customer service. He is just the type of person we need at Cellular One." He asked me to come into his office to chat.

Two weeks later, I was hired as retail manager of the Technical Services Department. Six months and two days later, I was promoted to regional technical service manager with technical responsibilities in forty-one stores. I reported to Steve. If I had not provided exceptional customer service to Mr. Smith at the department store, my career would have gone in a different direction. I'm glad that event happened from a career-progression perspective and because I had the distinct honor of working for Steve.

As I look back on my last twenty-one years in the corporate environment, Steve was by far the best boss I've had the honor of working for. He is a brilliant man. He's a man of integrity and faith. *Loyalty* means something to him. We worked hard, and he took care of his team.

The pivotal point in my life was a result of activating unwavering faith. My job situation did not show any progression until I removed fear and doubt from my life. When I started to operate in faith, doors and opportunities started to open for me. Faith and fear are like oil and water—they just don't mix. If fear is present, then faith is absent.

No matter what your situation looks like, if you want it to change, *you* have to make it happen. Before I went to work at Cellular One, I started to enjoy working in ladies' shoes—not because it was where I wanted to be but because it was where I needed to be at the time. If you find yourself stuck in a job you don't like and feel there is something better for you, don't give up. Continue to prepare yourself for the promotion because it will come. Learn to appreciate the job you have now. If you want to get promoted or get a new job, the key is to exercise your faith, master your current job, and be the best at what you do to the point where people really depend on you. Managers like hiring the go-to person!

Lessons Learned

1. When we don't have anyone to encourage us, we must encourage ourselves.

2. Faith requires patience and holding on—even when times seem impossible

3. God took me back to basics after my military career.

4. He did because I had to undergo basic training in the corporate world—just as I had to experience basic training at the beginning of my military career. As a result, I far exceeded expectations in both phases of my career. The pain was well worth the gain.

5. If you want to get promoted to a new job, you need to master and excel in your current job. Who wants to hire a poor performer?

6. The pivotal point came about in my life as a result of activating unwavering faith.

7. Living in the past will hinder you from progressing in the future.

8. Make sure you are a walking resume.

9. Enjoy your job because if you don't, someone else will.

10. If you are not generating results at work, what are you generating...at work?

CHAPTER

ANGELS IN THE PARKING LOT

When we look at our lives, we may not believe we have anything to be thankful for because we often base our success on material things, which causes us not to see the big picture. I have been guilty of it over and over again, and I have found myself having to repent for not being grateful for what I have and what I have accomplished. I am also guilty of living in the past, dwelling on material things I once had, and wondering where it all went. However, when I stop and take an assessment of my life, I have much more now than I had then since material things mean nothing in the Kingdom of Heaven. I can't take money or possessions with me.

This great testimony tells how the Holy Spirit used His great power to cause me to perform a task in an emergency. The Holy Spirit is so powerful and intelligent that I can hardly comprehend the awesomeness of His power. I have just touched the tip of the iceberg of greatness that is in store for me.

When I returned to the United States in 1985, I was reassigned to George Air Force Base in California, which was one my bases of preference. For some reason, when I arrived there, I had an overwhelming urge to become certified as a cardiopulmonary resuscitation (CPR) instructor. I got settled at my new duty station and mastered my new job. It was new for me to work at a base level or non-headquarters-level position. All my previous assignments were at the headquarters level.

I enjoyed my squadron and my team. After a few months, I decided to enroll in the CPR classes. I really loved teaching others. By becoming certified as a CPR instructor, I could teach classes and certify others as well.

After a week of really fun, informative classes, I became certified with the American Heart Association. I really liked having the knowledge, and I was thrilled about teaching the courses to others. However, I wondered if I would remember all the steps required to save a person's life if I ever had to use CPR on a person. A series of questions like that entered my mind, but I quickly dismissed them because they would lead to fear. My objective was to keep the faith so I could perform CPR the way I was taught to do so.

I remained certified throughout my seven years in California. I was eventually reassigned to Holloman Air Force Base in New Mexico for a couple of years before my retirement. I retired from the United States Air Force in January 1994 and moved to Montgomery. While I started in the cellular wireless telecommunications industry, I continued to work on my master's degree at Troy State University. Montgomery was very close to Selma, and we were quite pleased to stay in Montgomery during my transition from the military.

In 1996, I taught Sunday school classes to fifth and sixth graders. Our pastor was a man of tremendous knowledge, faith, and wisdom. He taught us to follow our hearts, pursue our dreams, and not let stumbling blocks get in our way. On one particular Sunday afternoon, my wife, daughter, and I were going through our traditional Sunday search and debate over where we were going to have lunch after church.

My son was married at the time, and he and his family attended a different church. My eight-year-old daughter informed us that we never considered her suggestions for Sunday lunch and was not going to give any input. As a result, we decided to go wherever she wanted to go for lunch. She said she wanted to go the Asian restaurant on Vaughn Road in East Montgomery. We told her it was a good choice and pointed our Dodge Caravan in the direction of the restaurant.

The sun was bright, and the temperature was at least ninety-five. When we pulled into the parking lot, people were standing over a man on the ground in a pool of blood. A man who turned out to be a fellow member of the United States Air Force was leaning over the man and pumping on his chest. After seeing what was going on, I stopped the van and ran toward the victim.

I stopped in my tracks, turned around, and went back to the van to get a pair of rubber gloves. I asked my wife to call 911. I ran toward the injured person as questions ran through my mind. *What if he is already dead? What if he dies in my arms? What if I don't remember what to do when I get there?* I felt as if my life was no longer my own, and the only thing that mattered at that moment was getting this man breathing again.

The Holy Spirit took control of my body in order to get a job done by giving me the gift of healing for that specific incident. The guy working on the victim asked if I knew CPR because he didn't. I told him I did, and I offered to take over the resuscitation.

The gentleman was bleeding heavily from his head, and his face and tongue were purple—and quickly turning of a deeper shade of purple. He was not breathing and looked like he was dead. All my CPR training came back to me like I was reading the instructions from a manual.

I told one of the ladies to get an umbrella and hold it over us as I started my procedures. My first task was to get the airway cleared of any obstruction so we could get him breathing again. One of the things I learned in training was that you take the risk of being bitten by the person as a natural reflex when you clear a person's throat. When I looked into his mouth, I saw food debris. I immediately put my finger into his mouth to clear as much as I could, and just as the book stated, he bit me. I was so glad to get a reaction from him.

As I cleared his throat, I saw vomit obstructing his airway. After I totally cleared his throat, I applied the Heimlich maneuver. My victim was unconscious, and I had to kneel astride the victim's thighs and place my fists between the bottom of his breastbone and his navel. I executed a series of sharp compressions by pushing inward and upward, but after the second compression, he moaned and coughed.

Since he had started breathing, CPR was not necessary. Just as he came around and started to breathe, the emergency medical team showed up, took control of the scene, and took the man to the hospital. During the entire ordeal, which lasted about five minutes, my motions, movements, and actions were totally controlled by the Holy Spirit. I knew exactly what to do and when to do it. I had total faith and confidence. I had no fear at all because I knew what it took to get that man breathing again.

We discovered the name of the person whose life God spared after we made some phone calls. Mr. Bechtel wrote an article in the *Montgomery Advertiser* about his near–death experience and how he was so thankful for the angels in the parking lot who came to his rescue.

Lessons Learned

1. Always follow your heart and pursue your dreams.
2. Take some time to stop and listen to what your children are saying. They have words of wisdom as well.
3. If you have an opportunity to help someone, please do so because you will be blessed each time.
4. When you convince yourself that you can be successful, the sky is the limit.
5. Life is extremely precious—whether it's your life or someone else's life. Don't judge others in need—assist others in need.
6. No matter how invincible we make ourselves out to be, we still need to rely on the assistance of others consistently.
7. Life is short so be thankful for each morning you rise.
8. What have you done for yourself lately?
9. What have you done for someone else lately?
10. There are times in our life when that little voice in our head really makes sense.

8 PEOPLE ARE GOD'S ANSWER TO ALL PROBLEMS

God inspired this chapter—and this entire book. I hope my readers can relate to some of the things I've expressed in the form of my testimonies. I dedicate this chapter to a young lady who refused to be defeated by the disappointments of this world. She is a woman of integrity and a strong survivor. My testimonies are real and true accounts of actual events that took place in my life, and I believe my testimonies should be shared with my readers, especially those who can relate to some or all the testimonies.

This book is based on seeking out men and women of integrity with the intention of helping them build personal character and have belief or faith in everything they set their minds to do. I refer to *integrity* in various chapters of this book because it takes a man or woman of character and integrity to totally operate in faith. I build and rebuild my personal character on a daily basis by doing my best to overcome any stumbling blocks.

A man or woman of integrity should take a personal inventory on a daily basis. We should always be conscious of how we spend our time here on earth because time is a gift. We spend most of our time being concerned about the things we cannot change. I will be the first to raise my hands and say I am guilty of dwelling on the things I don't have the power to change instead of focusing on the things I do have control over, such as the things I can do to make life better for my family and myself.

Sometimes we fall into our own little self-pity foxholes because we think and blame others like our families and friends for our problems in life. Actually, the real problem might be within us. My wife told me to stop beating myself up and focus on what's in front of me instead of focusing on the past. It is easy to let self-pity or low self-esteem become a normal way of life when we let life take a big chunk out of our backsides. It has to end at some point. If we think negatively about ourselves, we act in the same manner. If we think positively, pat ourselves on our shoulders, and focus on pleasant thoughts, we can change our attitudes from negative to positive and create a brighter future for ourselves and those we love.

We are always making plans for the future, but we really don't know what the future has in store for us. We often go through life filled with problems, pain, anger, and hard work. Before you know it, you get old and wonder what happened to your life.

People often say that if they were twenty years younger and knew what they know today, they would be in a much better position financially. This means that we often measure success by the numbers in our bank accounts. I have been guilty of this, and when I look back on my life, I wonder how much quality time I lost by thinking about what I could have been or should have been.

Some people measure success by their possessions, status, and jobs. I wonder if you can really measure success or if success can really be measured. A level of success for one person may or may not be enough for someone else. I believe success is not measured by a person's status; success in my book is measured by how well we overcome our falls and stumbling blocks. Success is measured by how fast we rise from a fall, brush off the dirt, hold our heads high, and walk like we own the world.

A person of integrity should understand we are only on this earth for a short time. We should seek to use our time as responsible people, and more importantly, we should seek to use our time wisely. Ladies and gentlemen, life is too short to gamble it away by dealing with foolish things. We don't have time for foolishness during our short time on earth. I have gambled with my life too often, and it is only by the grace and mercy of God that I am still alive.

When I say I am my own worst enemy, I find it most difficult to forgive myself for my mistakes and shortcomings. I find myself dwelling on the past and wondering what would have happened if I had changed my plan of action in certain situations. What if I had invested in bonds instead of stocks? What if I had not purchased some of the things I did and focused on saving more?

These things—and many more—will enter our thoughts daily if we let them, but we have to stop and call a time-out so we can take control of the game we play over and over in our minds. We need to learn to trust ourselves more and take the first step of admitting we have weaknesses. For example, I will never lose weight if I never convince myself I am overweight. I am responsible for what goes into my body, and I am responsible for taking care of my body.

Recently, a friend and coworker and I completed a run/walk fund-raiser. I told him I would feel a lot better about myself if I could get rid of my lunch box I carry around called my stomach. He told me if I stopped putting things in my lunch box, I wouldn't have to worry about having to carry it around. Although we spoke about it in a joking manner, those words never left me. We get out of life just what we deposit into life. It only takes a spark to get a flame going when you want to do the right thing for yourself. We must feel good about ourselves, pamper ourselves, and sometimes treat ourselves like kings and queens because we are descendants of royalty.

Another thing I learned over the years is that we must have patience. Things will not always work out the way we expect them to, and most of the time, things will work out better than we expect them to—but we must exercise patience. When I taught customer-service classes at my former company, I told my students to have patience with the customers and to listen to their side of the story before coming to any conclusions.

One of my best friends, Dr. Oggs, once said the customer is not necessarily always right. Sometimes the customer is misinformed and says or acts on what they were told. That's a true statement, and I will never forget it because I've been misinformed or misunderstood about many things. My frustration level rises to the top, causing me to think I have failed. I feel sad and alone. In reality, no matter what challenges we face in life, we should know we are not alone.

Earlier in this chapter, I talked about success and how people measure their levels of success. I want to live a life and present a positive attitude that others will want to emulate.

One of my former students recently went through a terrible ordeal in her life, and the ordeal really tested her faith. I dedicate this chapter to her. During the dark times in her life, she felt as if she could no longer put her trust in man. She had to put her trust in God. We talked from time to time, and I would check in with her occasionally to see how she was doing. She told me there were times when she decided to give up because the pain and pressure were too much to bear.

I had been on the road for several weeks as the new director of purchasing and inventory. Although I was no longer the call center director, I still checked on my former team. As soon as I got back to my office, I had a nagging urge to go to the call center to see my old team. My schedule was packed, and I decided to just go the floor and wave to everyone since it was an open floor. The young lady I am writing about was getting up from her seat just as I entered the room. I looked at her specifically, and we made eye contact. I smiled and waved at her, and she waved back at me with a winning smile before she sat down.

I went back to my office and thought nothing of it until she approached me several days later. When I saw her getting up from her seat, she was going to the ladies' room to end her life. When she saw my smile, something came over her and changed her mind instantly. She was about to give in to fear, but my smile gave her the faith to press on and not take what she thought was the easy way out. Until she spoke those words to me, I never knew God allowed my smile to save a person's life.

She had to be very strong to endure all the things she did because she never wore her pain on her face. That beautiful woman always maintained a beautiful smile, but deep inside, she was really hurting.

One afternoon, she asked if she could talk with me after work. I agreed, and we talked for about two hours. I mostly did the listening while she talked because she needed to vent some of her frustrations. I was a refreshing and listening ear for her. After we talked, I prayed for her and asked for God's blessing upon her life. I didn't see her for a long time, but I received e-mail from her.

Subject: With Great Appreciation!

T. J.

I wanted to take the time to let you know that I'm doing better. I went through a few life-impacting things this past year. There were times when I truly did not think I was going to make it. There were times I didn't want to make it. During that time, I often thought of those who were praying for me. Today, I wanted you to know you were one of those people. I view you as a wonderful, Godly, fathering person. You always seem extremely happy and willing to help anyone in need. Your thoughtfulness and professionalism are phenomenal. The day I came over and you took the time to talk, pray, minister, listen, help, and just be there when I needed someone will never be forgotten. I want to thank you for allowing God to use you to save me. I was truly lost and could not see the greatness before me. Since that day, things have not changed much. I, however, have. God has given me the strength to go on. My way of thinking has changed about a lot of things and the way that I view my life. Thank you for allowing me to open up and be honest with another human being again. I will never forget the time you spent with me. I appreciate your time and faithfulness to God. I truly felt that you understood. Your wonderful gestures and acts of kindness are probably just second nature to you, and it's a good possibility you have forgotten that day. Nevertheless, I cannot and will not forget. Thank you for just being you. You may wonder why I'm sending a thank you now. Well, it is simple. I made it! I realize how beautiful life is! I understand, through life, we all will experience a storm! I know God will always bring us out! And I know we are all here for a purpose! My pain and my suffering were for my growth. You took the time, and I just want to thank you. I have already thanked God for you and others, but I feel I owed it to you to let you know how great a gift you were for me. T. J., thanks for being that father when I could/would not go to my own! You are a wonderful person! Thank you for being the needed shoulder for my tears!

May God's blessings continue to shower you and your loved ones! Have a wonderful week!

Thanks for your time!

Sincerely,
T. A.

When life throws challenges and curves our way, we must be prepared to take them head-on and with the mindset we will survive. The things T. A. spoke about in her e-mail are in the past now, and she is moving on with her life. My recent conversation with her convinced me she is on fire and crushing the enemy whenever he shows his ugly head. For her, the past is the past—and we must understand that we cannot change the past. We need to let go of the past so we can enjoy the gifts that are waiting for us in the present and future.

Dealing with the enemies we have is difficult enough—let's not continue to create more problems by becoming our own worst enemy. I have come to the realization that I am a dragon slayer, but I also know that some dragons are not meant for me to slay them. I am not alone in this game, and I must keep faith on my side and in the forefront of my life. We have no room for doubt and fear in our lives. We must rely on faith. Just as T. A. overcame her fears, got up from being knocked down, brushed off the sand, and held her head up high, so can you. God will always put a person in your life for a season to solve a particular problem.

Lessons Learned

1. We should always be conscious of how we spend our time on earth because time is a precious gift that you can never get back.
2. Don't let self-pity or low-esteem become our normal way of life.
3. If we think negatively about ourselves, we often respond in the same manner.

4. Success is measured by how fast we rise from a fall, brush off the dirt, hold our heads high, and walk like we own the world.

5. A simple smile is all it takes to make someone's day or save someone's life.

6. Most people hear, but few people really listen.

7. At the end of each day try adding up all of your hits and misses. Are you happy with your score?

8. Who's watching you? What example are you setting?

9. How do you know if you are adding value?

10. Words hurt, words help, words heal, words matter!

9
IT'S NOT WHAT YOU KNOW—IT'S WHO YOU KNOW

A person's character includes integrity, courage, discipline, vision, endurance, and compassion. One really important aspect of character is a good reputation. Your reputation goes ahead of you. Reputation is a word that stands alone because of its many meanings. What do I care about my reputation? What do *you* care about my reputation? I've lived with those questions throughout my life. I often asked myself if having a good reputation really mattered, and I discovered it does matter. There are people with good reputations and some with bad reputations.

Can you name ten people you know with good reputations? I'm sure you can without doubt or hesitation—or can you? How do you attain a good reputation? Sometimes we associate with other people with good reputations, and it makes us look good. Maybe our parents have status in the community, and we latch onto their status and good reputation just by having the family name.

One's reputation goes beyond the personal realm, and it ventures out into the business world. Companies will spend big bucks branding their products because the business they get is well worth it. If customers trust a company's reputation, they will surely open their wallets, pay more for a product, take a chance on new products, and be more loyal to the company. People have a tendency to be more forgiving of occasional mistakes if a company has a history of integrity.

When my family and I travel, we make reservations at the same chain of hotels all the time because of its reputation. When we fly, we use the same airline because of its reputation. When you stop to look at it, reputation, especially a good reputation, is a part of just about everything we do. It affects most of our decisions. We want to spend our money at restaurants with good reputations and bank with reputable banks. Sometimes we choose our friends based on their reputations.

The reputation I strive to maintain in my daily life is most important to me. First of all, I want to keep a good reputation as a man of integrity. I also want to have a good reputation with my fellow man and woman in my everyday roster of activities. People are impressed by others who possess those types of characteristics, and people are blessed as well. My reputation and positive attitude have caused me to receive substantial blessings and be a blessing to others. In life, we go from not enough to just enough to more than enough.

My testimony deals with character and good reputation. I have been working in the wireless telecommunications industry for many years. In this industry, like other large and fast-moving industries, you always have to be ready for change. I've gone through two major company purchases, including downsizing.

Throughout all these mergers, downsizings, and purchases, God has shown favor and allowed me to maintain employment.

During a corporate merger, I was faced with having to leave the company because there were no more positions for me to apply for. I applied for several positions within the company, but I was never selected. Finally, I interviewed for a great position as a project manager as a result of being recommended based on my ability to do the job, past performances, and my character and good reputation. The hiring manager indicated my reputation preceded me, and it was a huge plus, but the funding was not available at the time.

On a Friday afternoon, the hiring manager called to let me know I had been selected for the position. However, due do a lack of funding, they were not able to make me an offer. I had already received my severance briefing, and I had one more week before I was to be considered officially unemployed for the first time in ten years. I was devastated, but I had to stay focused on making progress and not letting the enemy get the best of me.

I was angry with myself because I had no one else to blame. I felt anger toward the system because I felt the system was letting me down. The system did not take into consideration all my hard work, and the system didn't care about me as a person. I was only thought of as a number. These crazy thoughts entered my mind daily, and they became more real as my countdown to unemployment continued. I appreciated the phone call from the person who was to be my new boss. Having a lack of funds for this position goes far beyond the scope of the hiring manager, so he was surely not to blame. The position had been funded from the start of the acquisition of the project, but at the last minute, the project was forced to close, which was after I had been given the green light to start.

On Sunday, my family and I went to church as we do every Sunday. On that particular Sunday in August 2003, the sermon dealt with reexamining our hearts. It was a sermon I needed to hear because I had been blaming the system for not getting a job after the merger. Fear took control. I was afraid of the unknown. I had to go back into the job market after being employed for so long. I should have never let fear set in, and I should have never blamed the system for my errors. After hearing such a powerful sermon, I did just as the pastor told us to do. I went home, found a secret place, and prayed for forgiveness for blaming others for my problems when in reality the problem resided within me.

In our new home, we have a room that was designated from the foundation to be our prayer room. I went to our prayer room and prayed to God to forgive me for being hard-hearted toward a system that had nothing to do with my situation. My fear of potentially not being employed went away, and my faith took control of the situation.

On Monday, I went to work for what was to be my last workweek with the company. I really hated to leave the company because it is a great company with great benefits, great pay, and great people. How could I find a better company to work for than the one I was with? As I went into what was to be my last staff meeting with one of the greatest bosses in the world, he pulled me aside and said, "I have great news. You will not have to look for employment outside this company. There is a job waiting for you."

As he was talking to me, my phone vibrated. When I retrieved the message, the hiring manager told me funding for the position had miraculously reappeared. Funding was nowhere to be found on

Friday, but something happened over the weekend. The funding was now available. I wonder what happened over the weekend.

Lessons Learned

1. Maintaining a good reputation and always exercising integrity will open doors for you that were once closed.
2. In life, we go from not enough to just enough to more than enough.
3. It's easy to blame the system. Maybe we should consider taking inventory of our own actions.
4. When you find yourself in situations that seem devastating, it's important to remain focused.
5. If someone says your reputation precedes you, should you be worried or flattered?
6. Your reputation is your brand.
7. It's not what you know, it's who you know, as long as who you know, knows what you know.
8. Ask someone to honestly describe you in three words. Are you happy with the answers?
9. Honestly describe yourself in three words. Are you happy with the answers?
10. Who's in control of you? What's in control of you?

CHAPTER

10

MY PERSPECTIVE: ACTIVATING YOUR FAITH

I've been working on this book for years, and I often wondered why I wasn't able to complete the last chapter. Well, now I know why it took so long. The last chapter of the book was waiting on the present phase in my life.

After spending twenty-one years in the corporate world, I've experienced my share of agony and victory. We've heard about the thrill of victory and the agony of defeat on numerous occasions. In my world, with every accomplishment of victory, we experience some aspect of agony. I call it the peak-and-valley syndrome. We all go through peaks and valleys as we live and breathe. The peaks are thrilling, but the valleys are chilling. My objective is to share testimonials and examples of how to overcome the valleys. If we are not prepared, we will find ourselves camping out in the valleys of disappointment for far too long.

My corporate career started four months after I retired from the United States Air Force. I enjoyed twenty years, four months, and twenty-one days of serving my country. I thoroughly enjoyed my Air Force career from start to finish. I started to get depressed as I approached the end of my career, which is probably normal for most career military personnel. I still remember the last day I wore my Air Force uniform.

I knew life would be different for my family and me as we embarked on a new adventure, seeking a new career in the corporate world. My transition between the military and the civilian life was extremely hard—mentally and physically. People say, "Looking for a job is a job."

I experienced it personally. I got up each morning at the same time as I did for twenty years. I got dressed and pursued my dream of going to work in a corporate environment, traveling, and making lots of money. That was my dream and my daily prayer.

Let's talk about faith and fear in this scenario. I was scared out of my mind because I didn't have an income with the exception of my Air Force retirement pension, which was just about enough to keep food on the table for my family. I had faith that I would land the ideal job in the right company, but I had no clue about what company I would be working for—or the city or the state. I learned from experience that I could not operate in faith and fear at the same time. I would vacillate between faith and fear throughout the day, but fear dominated most my time. I was afraid of the unknown.

Twenty-one years later, as I write the last chapter, I find myself in the same situation. My corporate position was impacted, eliminated, taken away, deleted, and vanished—just like that! I was informed early November in 2015 that my last day would be December 31, 2015. I had the opportunity to seek another position within the company, but I was led to take the severance package and start something new. Although I wasn't the only person impacted, it was a total life changing experience. The only difference between my transitions from the military to civilian life as compared to my transition from a corporate environment to whatever is next is that I am not operating in fear! I am operating in total and complete faith. As I write this last chapter, I've been out of work for five months and twenty-two days—and I'm just fine.

Let me take you back to 1994 and share my experiences about how to survive, progress, and excel in the corporate environment. Just as I thoroughly enjoyed my military career, I also had an awesome twenty-one years in the corporate wireless industry. Did I have twenty-one years of work, tasks, and projects with no issues or problems? Absolutely not!

After retiring from the Air Force, I relocated my family back to Selma for thirty days. We lived with my mother-in-law during the transition. I really had no intentions of working anywhere else in the country because I had my sights set on moving to Selma. My family and I spent December in Selma, but on January 2, we put gas in the Dodge Caravan and hit the road, looking for work in Selma or Montgomery.

I went to a temp agency in Montgomery to get registered. I thought they would assist me in finding a job, but I was treated like a criminal instead of a veteran. I'm certain they threw my application in the trash as soon as I left the office. I could feel the resentment from them, and it was very cold. The staff spent no time interviewing me and didn't show any interest in me whatsoever. After spending about thirteen minutes in the office, I departed in disappointment.

While living with my mother-in-law, I sent out more than four hundred résumés. The job of selling shoes landed me a job with

Cellular One—thanks to God sending an angel in my direction. Steve was instrumental in getting me started in my wireless career, and I am forever grateful to him then, now, and for the rest of my life. He was by far the most intelligent, professional, and caring boss I've worked for in my life. Everything he did was totally first class. He is a man of integrity, and his leadership skills were impeccable. Some days, while working for Steve, because of the nature of my job, I put in some very long days. I had no problem because he worked just as hard and as long as we did.

My career moved me from retail service manager in Montgomery to regional service manager. I served as manager for all our retail service departments. Later, I became call center manager and call center director. From there, I was promoted to director of purchasing, inventory, and training.

When a Fortune 50 wireless company purchased our company in 2002, my responsibilities changed. The culture was very different from what we were accustomed to, which was a result of migrating from hundreds of employees to thousands of employees. Between 2002 and 2015, I was associate director, manager, and senior consultant. I faced excellent times and challenging times. The problems will come and go like the rain. The challenge is knowing how to overcome those challenges and move forward. Also, the challenge is knowing how to sustain the impact when you are in the midst of a storm with more storms in the queue.

Of all the positions I held, I was most passionate about career development. I believe the legacy I will leave in the corporate industry will be a legacy of career development. I've had the pleasure of teaching many career-development classes that benefited my audience—and me. I have a passion for seeing young leaders progressing in their careers by working hard and getting promoted.

I had the honor of orchestrating and leading future leader classes from 2006 to 2015. I witnessed coordinators migrating from frontline positions to elevated leadership positions. I was most proud when I saw the organizational announcement communicating the promotion of one of our future leaders. I take it personally. When you spend five to seven months with a class of ten young and eager minds, you see them excel and grow. It's very rewarding to see them get promoted. The promotion rate was substantial for these young leaders once they graduated. Some were promoted prior to graduation from the program because they were so marketable based on experience, customer service, drive, and ambition.

Dealing with Leaders in the Workplace

I am not sure if I will ever understand why people feel as if they own the company when their names are not on the company's brand. In a corporate environment, all employees own a small piece of the company as a result of dedication and hard work. Leaders have bosses too, but they treat people as if they are the company. Don't treat your employees as if the sun rises and sets on *you* each day.

I've had great bosses in my career, and I've had some interesting bosses in the workplace—both male and female. Leaders often try to manage people, and that's not how the world works. As a leader, I was trained to lead people, but I was not trained to manage people. I can effectively manage money, I can manage time, and I can manage things, but I can't manage people because people have brains. If you know how to properly lead people, the people you lead will go well above and beyond the call of duty. They will be successful. If the team is successful, the leader will be extremely successful.

How do you deal with interesting bosses? The first thing is to not let them get under your skin. You must have really thick skin to properly operate and survive in the corporate world. In my mind, leaders who treat you like dirt and lead with fear are leaders who look for teams to respond in fear. In my mind, the worst mistake you can make is to let them instill fear in your life. The enemy will always win as long as they know you are terrified and operate in fear. They thrive on operating in fear.

When you fear the enemy, you add fuel to the fire—and they win. A barking dog will seem extremely ferocious as long as the dog is shielded from you. Remove the barrier—and see if that dog acts the same way. They will have a different approach because you are in a position to confront them. I am not saying to disrespect or confront your boss, but you need to let your boss know you are a living and breathing person—just as they are—and you both breathe the same air. In other words, your boss needs to treat you with dignity and respect if they want respect.

During my twenty-one years of corporate experience, my first boss was a very popular guy. He was the one who gave me my first job in cellular as a result of selling him shoes. He was fair and funny. He made the atmosphere and the workplace fun. Although wireless devices were new to us, we had lots of customers who wanted to talk all day and night, but they wanted low bills at the end of the month. He knew how to handle irate customers who threatened to demolish the retail store. He was a great golfer and a great negotiator. He was known throughout the city, and it was a plus for us. He treated his employees with respect and made the time to listen to their concerns. His leadership style was to instill love and not fear. We worked hard, but we really wanted to be present in the workplace.

As manager, he would sometimes make promises to customers and not inform me of those promises in a timely manner. When those customers approached and said, "Your boss promised me you will have my cell phone and the hands-free kit installed in my car today with no appointment necessary," I had to bite my lip and make it happen. Why did I make those exceptions? First of all, I needed to keep the customers happy, honor my boss's promises, and maintain self-control. I learned several key attributes from him, but my takeaway was that he loved his customers—and his customers loved him. His customer-friendly personality caused us to make our store extremely successful.

I am not going to share my entire twenty-one-year corporate history of good, bad, and ugly bosses. However, I have to talk about my favorite leader again. Steve was the reason I was introduced to the wireless industry. He saw my résumé, was intrigued by it, and made the decision to meet with me for an informal interview. After working for six months in the retail industry, I was promoted by faith. I applied for a regional manager's job within the company after having been on the job for only four months. My coworkers thought I was insane to apply for a new job within the company in less than one year. According to the hiring rules of the company, I could not apply for a new position within the company until I'd been in position for at least six months. I politely informed my coworkers that I wasn't eligible to move to a new position for six months, but nothing in the rulebook said I couldn't apply for a new job in less than six months. I activated my faith by focusing on one job, knowing beyond a shadow of a doubt that I was going to get that job strictly on faith. My coworkers bugged me daily about the status of my application. I said, "I haven't heard anything yet, but the job is mine. It's just a matter of time."

On my six-month anniversary with the company, I heard nothing about my application. After having been with the company for six months and two days, Steve called and scheduled me for an interview. I was promoted to regional manager a week later. That's what I call faith in action!

Steve goes down in my corporate history book as the very best boss, manager, and leader I've ever had the pleasure of working for and with. He was caring, passionate about his team, and the best negotiator I've ever seen. I categorize him as brilliant! As a result of learning so much from Steve, I was able to build a solid foundation for the remainder of my corporate career. When I was in horrible situations on the job, I often asked myself, "What would Steve do in a situation like this?" By asking this simple question, I was able to withstand a multitude of fiery darts from the enemy as I progressed in my career.

Some bosses hate you, talk bad about you behind your back, or curse you to your face. They will do their best to make your life a living hell. They will lie, cheat, and try their best to set you up for failure. I don't believe it has anything to do with race or religious beliefs. I believe some are just plain angry all the time. Fortunately, I only had three bosses I could categorize as crazy or angry! Although the experiences were extremely unpleasant, I learned to never mistreat or disrespect my employees.

When I progressed up the corporate ladder, I could expect to encounter some turbulence. Although I reached cruising altitude in my career, I was always prepared for turbulence. The key takeaway was being prepared for turbulence.

How to Survive Corporate Turbulence: TJ-ology

1. Always work to stay two steps ahead of your boss. It comes naturally once you get a good understanding of your boss and his or her hot buttons.

2. Know what business you are in at all times (customer service). If you are in business for yourself or working in a business for someone else, your reason for being in business is to satisfy the customer. Without the customer, there's no business. When you mistreat the customer, both internal and external, you may as well go home.

3. Know your job extremely well—and take on an attitude of constant learning. Learn as much as you can as often as you can.

4. Arrive at work ahead of your boss and leave with your boss or shortly thereafter.

5. If possible, don't make a habit of responding to e-mails from your boss late at night because he or she will expect it to be the norm.

6. Get enough rest each night so you will be on top of your game daily.

7. Ensure you have work that's meaningful and substantial where you can measure your success and add value to the department and company. You must be able to show a return on investment from the work you do. No matter how well you do your job, there is always room for improvement.

8. Be innovative and creative—consistently. Never get stuck in a vacuum. If you know your business well, you should

be able to take advantage of technology to create or invent methodology for improvements.

9. Always go to staff meetings or business meetings prepared. Know your numbers and your key performance indicators daily (and hourly if necessary).

10. Know your targets and what is needed to reach those targets. If you don't reach your targets daily, weekly, or monthly, you need to know why and have a plan for improvement. If you reach your targets consistently, your goals may be too low. Always incorporate stretch goals to push yourself and your team to reach new goals.

Getting Passed Over for Promotion when You Know You Are Qualified

Looking at the beginning of my career and the end of my career, there is no comparison. I am not sure if it's a sign of the times or just the nature of the people you work for. When I started my career in 1994, promotions were based on the ability to do the job and the effort you put into making a successful career. I am sure there were instances where people were not promoted based on some type of secret system, but I never experienced that early in my career. As a baby boomer, my generation believes in a hard day's work equals honest compensation. I could never say my compensation wasn't commensurate with my work, but pay isn't everything when you look at the big picture. I was fortunate in my career to have been blessed with some leaders who played fairly.

What do you do when you feel you have been passed over for positions you know you were qualified for?

a. Ask for honest and candid feedback from the hiring manager about why you were not considered for the position. Please don't settle for textbook answers. "You were very close to being considered, but we found someone who was more qualified and already doing the job." You may also get generic letters. "Thank you for applying for the job. You didn't get the job, but we will keep your application on file."

b. Consult your immediate supervisor to work on your behalf for collecting constructive feedback for you.

c. It is not wise to apply for a job without informing your immediate supervisor because your supervisor will be notified when you apply for a position. In some instances, your immediate supervisor must approve the application before it's actually submitted. Your immediate supervisor may also get a call or an e-mail to verify your employment or verify if you are qualified for the position based on current or past performance. Get your supervisor involved when you are applying for a job, and get their buy-in, recommendation, and approval.

d. If you don't have a mentor, get one. Find someone you trust and feel comfortable with to manage your career as your mentor. It's possible to have more than one mentor during your career. A mentor is someone who will take on the responsibility of monitoring and managing your career. A mentor knows what you know and should be in a position to tell you when to apply for a position.

e. Finally, do all you can to prepare yourself. Don't tell everyone your plans for career development because you will get those who will try to discourage you by saying you are not qualified simply because they don't want to see you advance in your career. Narrow down your job search opportunities to two or three, and focus on those. If you know what you want to do next in your career, you shouldn't be all over the place. Stay focused and know that every no response moves you one step closer to a yes.

Understanding Your Boss

In my career, I've learned to trust very few people in the workplace. In the corporate world, we all have a boss or more than one boss. Work hard to establish a professional relationship with your boss. Determine what you have in common: habits, traits, sports, or books. Put yourself in his or her place, and ask yourself what you would do differently. If your responses to yourself are significant and will add value to the business, diplomatically share your thoughts with your boss if possible.

1. Never say anything bad about your boss—whether you like him or her or not.
2. Always treat your boss with dignity and respect—even if you are not getting the same from him or her.
3. You should know your job and always do it well.
4. Meet deadlines, and keep your boss informed about all projects consistently.
5. Never let your boss ask you for status updates. Provide updates proactively.

6. If you ever plan to go over your boss's head to complain about anything, inform your boss of your plans.

7. Never send an e-mail to your boss's boss without informing or sending a courtesy copy to your immediate boss.

8. Always dress in a professional manner. Your company may already have a business casual policy or a casual policy. My personal recipe for corporate dress is to wear a suit and tie Monday through Thursday. Friday casual simply means I leave the tie in the car—just in case. If for some reason I wear jeans on Friday because of a special event, I have to add a blazer to the mix.

9. Never engage in negative conversations with another team member or anyone else in the organization about anyone in the company, especially your boss. It will come back to bite you sooner or later.

10. Keep busy throughout the day. There is no time for shooting the breeze in the corporate world. My first real job was at the age of fifteen as a bag boy in a supermarket in Selma. My store manager, Mr. Smith, said, "If you have time to lean, you have time clean!" There is always something to do in an organization.

Lessons Learned

Looking back on my career, I've been blessed. I've met some wonderful people and some questionable people. Through it all, it was a good ride. My faith was tested many times, and I've experienced my share of fear. When I walked in fear, I lost the battle every time. When I walked in faith during my career, I consistently hit home runs. If I had to repeat my corporate career, my strategic plan would be:

1. Always treat everyone with dignity and respect.
2. Get seven to eight hours of sleep each night.
3. Make it your business to look out for number one—and number one is you.
4. Make time for your family by practicing and exercising work-life balance.
5. If your company is willing to pay for your education, take full advantage of that benefit. If you don't, you will cheat yourself and regret it later in life.
6. Take advantage of any savings and retirement programs the company offers.
7. Be sure to commit to a regular exercise program and work out at least three times per week.
8. Read a book (or more) a month.
9. Become the heartbeat of the business.
10. Know your numbers (key performance indicators) consistently.

The Secret to Activating Your Faith

The activation of faith is simple. You *conceive* it, *believe* it, and *achieve* it.

Conceive: The conception process starts when you get an idea in your head.

Action: Define your goal and give birth to the idea by speaking it into existence.

Believe: Convince or persuade yourself that you *will* reach your goal.

Achieve: Create an action plan to achieve your goal. If you fail to plan, you plan to fail.

CONCLUSION

I've enjoyed writing this book. With God's blessing, this book will be the foundation for my pursuit of becoming a motivational teacher. Knowledge is the key to success in life because no one can take it away from you. Knowledge is power! Knowledge is simply getting educated about whatever you are looking for or working on. No matter what you attempt to do in life, always get an understanding first.

Lessons Learned

1. Always prepare yourself—no matter what situation you may be facing personally or professionally.
2. Finding a great mentor is better than striking gold.
3. Tap into your passion—and let it propel you toward your destiny.
4. Rejoice when others are promoted because they will do the same for you.
5. Your faith will open doors for you beyond your wildest imagination.
6. A very smart corporate executive vice president once told me, there are two endings in life. One is an end to

corporate and the other is the end of life. We should be
prepared for both because one day they will come.

7. You should always know the ingredients of your personal
brand.

8. I'm always concerned about who people say I am.

9. I strive to align my core values, my talent and my passion
with my brand.

10. When you fear the enemy, you add fuel to the fire and
the enemy wins. When you have FAITH, you add
CONFIDENCE to the mix and YOU WIN!!!

I conclude this book with a poem I wrote for my mother,
who was my inspiration from the day I was born until the day she
entered into the Kingdom of Heaven!

Mother, You Taught Me Well

When I was a child, you held me in your arms;
You vowed to protect me from all hurt and harm.
You read books to me while you taught me to read.
You taught me to follow and then taught me to lead.
You taught me to love and never to hate.
You taught me to be punctual and said, "Never be late"
You said knowledge is power and education is the key.
You said stay in school and be all you can be.
You taught me to work at an early stage;
I hated it then, but now I'm grateful with age.
I was never hungry or wore clothes with holes;
When my shoes were worn, you repaired my soles.
You said we may not have the best, but we were good to go.

You worked three jobs just to make it so.

You said take care of your family and make sure they eat.

Put clothes on their backs and shoes on their feet.

Mom, you gave your all, and you did all you could do;

You were not only Mom but the dad I never knew.

When I married my soul mate, Sheila, you shared my joy.

We gave you Oronde, a blessed baby boy!

Then we gave you Christa, the anointed delight!

Now five grandkids, what a joyful sight.

I will miss our conversations and the funnies you could tell.

You were awesome, Mother, and guess what?

You taught me very well!

Edwards Brothers Malloy
Thorofare, NJ USA
October 12, 2016